Guide to Programming and Algorithms Using R

Özgür Ergül

Guide to Programming and Algorithms Using R

 Springer

Özgür Ergül
Electrical and Electronics Engineering
Middle East Technical University
Ankara, Turkey

ISBN 978-1-4471-6204-9   ISBN 978-1-4471-5328-3 (eBook)
DOI 10.1007/978-1-4471-5328-3
Springer London Heidelberg New York Dordrecht

Dedication

```
01 dedicate = function(reader){
02    if (reader == mywife){
03        print("To my wife...")
04    }
05    else if (reader == myparents){
06        print("To my parents...")
07    }
08    else{
09        print("To all programmers...")
10    }
11 }
```

Preface

Computer programming is one of fundamental areas in engineering. As computers have permeated our modern lives, it has been increasingly more attractive to write programs to make these machines work for us. Only a couple of decades ago, a computer course was the first time that a student met with a computer. Today, a standard first-year undergraduate student has at least ten years of experience on using programs and diverse software on their desktops, laptops, and smart phones. But, interestingly, when it comes to writing programs in addition to using them, programming courses and materials considered in those mandatory practical hours remain as "difficult stuff" for many students, who are even experts in using their technological gadgets.

There are extremely many books in computer programming, some of which are excellent sources for teaching and learning programming and related concepts. Programming would be incomplete without explaining underlying algorithms. Hence, most of these books also cover algorithmic techniques for solving problems, which are usually accompanied by some coding techniques using a programming language or pseudocodes. I am also using various books in my own courses. Some of them contain hundreds of pages with nice discussions on programming and algorithms. On the other hand, I have witnessed that, when they have trouble to understand a concept or a part of material, many students prefer internet, such as discussion boards, rather than their books. Their responses to my question, i.e., why they are not willing to follow their books, has forced me to write this one, not to replace other texts in this area, but to support them via an introductory material that many student find quite easy to follow.

My discussions with students have often led to the same point that they admit what they find difficult while programming. I have found interesting that students are actually very successful to understand some critical concepts, such as recursion, that many lecturers and instructors consider difficult. On the other hand, they are struggling on implementing algorithms and writing their own programs because of some common mistakes. These "silly" mistakes, as called by students themselves, are not written in books, and they are difficult to solve since programming environments do not provide sufficient feedback on their mistakes. My reaction has been collecting these common mistakes and including them in course materials that have significantly boosted student performance. This book also contains such faulty programs written by students along with discussions for better programming.

When it comes to the point where I need to tell what is special about this book, I would describe it as a simple, concise, and short material that may be suitable for introductory programming courses. Some of the discussions in the text may be found as "stating the obvious" by many lecturers and instructors, but in fact, I have collected them from my discussions with students, and they actually include answers to those questions that students are often embarrassed to ask. I have also filtered topics such that only threshold concepts, which are major barriers in learning computer programming, are considered in this book. I believe that higher-level topics can easily be understood once the topics focused in this book are covered.

This book contains nine chapters. The first chapter is an introduction, where we start with simple examples to understand programming and algorithms. The second and third chapters present two important concepts of programming, namely loops and recursions. We consider various example programs, including those with mistakes that are commonly experienced by beginners. In the fourth chapter, we focus on the efficiency of programs and algorithms. This topic is unfortunately omitted or skipped fast in some programming courses and books, but in fact, it is required to understand why we are programming. Another important aspect, i.e., accuracy, is focused in the fifth chapter. A major topic in computer programming, namely, sorting is discussed in the sixth chapter, followed by the seventh chapter that is devoted to linear systems of equations. In the eighth chapter, we briefly discuss file processing, i.e., investigating and modifying simple files. Finally, the last chapter presents some mini projects that students may enjoy while programming.

As the title of this book suggests, all programs given in this book are written in the R language. This is merely a choice, which is supported by some of its favorable properties, such as being freely available and easy to use. Even though a single language is used throughout the book, no strict assumptions have been made so that all discussions are also valid for other programming languages. Except the last one, each chapter ends with a set of exercises that needs to be completed for fully understanding the given topics because programming and algorithms cannot be learned without evaluating, questioning, and discussing the material in an active manner via hands-on practices.

Enjoy it!

Ankara, Turkey   Özgür Ergül

Contents

Introduction

This introductory chapter starts with the programming concept, where we discuss various aspects of programs and algorithms. We consider a simple omelette-cooking algorithm to understand the basic principles of programming. Then, we list the common properties of computer programs, followed by some notes on programming in R, particularly by using the function concept. Finally, matrices and vectors, as well as their representations in R, are briefly discussed.

1.1 Programming Concept

A *computer program* is a sequence of commands and instructions to effectively solve a given problem. Such a problem may involve calculations, data processing, or both. Each computer program is based on an underlying procedure called *algorithm*. An algorithm may be implemented in different ways, leading to different programs using the same procedure. We follow this convention throughout this book, where an algorithm refers to a list of procedures, whereas a program refers to its implementation as a code.

A computer program is usually written by humans and executed by computers, as the name suggests. For the solution of a given problem, there are usually several programs and algorithms available. Some of them can be better than others considering the efficiency and/or accuracy of results. These two aspects should be defined now.

- Efficiency often refers to the speed of programs and algorithms. For example, one can measure the time spent for the solution of a given problem. The shorter the duration (processing time), the better the efficiency of the program and algorithm used. Note that this (being faster) is quite a relative definition that involves comparisons of multiple programs and algorithms. In some cases, memory required for the solution of a problem can be included in the definition of the efficiency. In such a case, using less memory is favorable, and a program/algorithm using relatively small amount of memory is called to be efficient. For both speed and memory usage, the efficiency of a program/algorithm naturally depends on its inputs.

Ö. Ergül, *Guide to Programming and Algorithms Using R*,
DOI 10.1007/978-1-4471-5328-3_1,
© Springer-Verlag London 2013

- When a program/algorithm is used, the aim is usually to get a set of results called *outputs*. Depending on the problem, outputs can be letters, words, or numbers. Accuracy is often an issue when dealing with numerical outputs. Since programs are implemented on computers, numerical results may not be exact, i.e., they involve errors. This is not because programs are incorrect, but because computers use floating-point representations of numbers, leading to rounding errors. Although being negligible one by one, rounding errors tend to accumulate and become visible in outputs. A program/algorithm that produces less error is called more accurate than other programs/algorithms that produce more errors. Obviously, similar to efficiency, accuracy is a relative property. But it is common to call a program/algorithm *stable* when it produces consistently accurate results under different circumstances, i.e., for different inputs.

When comparing programs and algorithms, there are usually tradeoffs between efficiency and accuracy. Hence, one may need to investigate a set of possible programs and algorithms in detail to choose the best of them for given requirements. This is also the main motivation in programming.

1.2   Example: An Omelette-Cooking Algorithm

Assume that we would like to write an algorithm for cooking a simple omelette and implement it as a program. As opposed to standard ones, these are to be executed by humans. Let us simply list the basic steps.

- Gather eggs, crack them in a cup.
- Use a fork to mix them.
- Add salt, mix again.
- Pour butter onto a pan.
- Put the heat on. Wait until the butter melts.
- Pour the egg mixture onto the pan.
- Wait until there is no liquid visible.

This list can be considered as a program, since it is a sequence of commands and instructions to effectively solve the omelette-cooking problem. Note that dividing the third item into two parts as

- Add salt.
- Mix again.

would lead to another program, even though the algorithm (the underlying procedure) would not change.

For this program to work smoothly, we need a cup, a fork, a pan, and heat. Under normal circumstances, these items do not change. Hence, they can be called the *constants* of the program. Of course, we can use a bowl instead of a cup to mix eggs. This is perfectly allowed, but constants are considered to be fixed in the content of the program, and changing them means modifying the program itself. Hence, using a bowl instead of a cup would be writing another program, which could be more suitable in some cases, e.g., for large numbers of eggs. Such a modification can be minor (using bowl instead of cup) or major (adding pepper after salt). Making modifications on purpose to change a program, in accordance with new needs or to make it better, can be simply interpreted as *programming*.

In addition to the constants defined above, we need eggs, salt, and butter in order to cook an omelette. These can be considered as the *inputs* of the program. These items and their properties tend to change in every execution. For example, the size of eggs will be different from omelette to omelette, but the program above (including constants) remains the same. Note that this is actually the idea behind programming: Programs are written while considering that they will be required and used for different inputs. Types and numbers of inputs are included in the process of programming and often chosen by the programmer who writes the program. In our case, one might consider the number of eggs as an input, which could be used to determine whether a cup or a bowl is required. This would probably extend the applicability of the program to more general cases.

Finally, in the program above, the omelette is the result, hence the output. Outputs and their properties (for example, the taste of the omelette in our case) depend on both constants and inputs, as well as operations performed in the program in accordance with the instructions given.

Now let us try to implement the omelette-cooking algorithm in a more systematic way. In this case, we use some signs to define operations. Let us also list constants, inputs, and outputs clearly. From now on, we use a `different` font to distinguish program texts from normal texts.

Constants: `cup, fork, heat, pan`
Inputs: `eggs, salt, butter`
- `egg_mixture = eggs → cup`
- `egg_mixture = fork > egg mixture`
- `egg_mixture = egg mixture + salt`
- `pan_content = butter → pan`
- `pan_content = pan_content + heat`
- `pan_content = pan_content + egg_mixture`
- `omelette = pan_content + heat`
Output: `omelette`

In this format, → represents crack/add/pour, > represents apply/use, + represents add/mix (including heating), and = represents update operations. Even though these are defined arbitrarily here, each programming language has its own set of rules and operations for writing programs.

Note how the steps are written in the revised format, especially using `egg_mixture` and `pan_content`. These two items are called the *variables* of the program. They vary depending on the inputs. The variable `egg_mixture` is first obtained by cracking `eggs` into `cup`. It is then updated by using `fork` and adding `salt`. The variable `pan_content` is first obtained by pouring `butter` into `pan`. It is then updated by adding `heat` and pouring `egg_mixture`, followed by adding further `heat` to produce the output, i.e., `omelette`. Similar to constants, but as opposed to inputs and outputs, variables of a program are not seen and may not be known by its users.

1.3   Common Properties of Computer Programs

It is now convenient to list some common properties of computer programs.
- Programs are usually written by humans and executed by computers. Hence, a program should be clear, concise, and direct.
- Programs are usually lists of consecutive steps. Hence, it is expected that a program has a flow in a certain direction, usually from top to bottom.
- Programs have well-defined initiations (where to start) and terminations (where to stop and extract output).
- Programs have well-defined constants, inputs, outputs, and variables.
- Programs are written by using a finite set of operations defined by programming languages. Any new operation can be written using default operations provided by the language.
- Each item (scalar, vector, or matrix) in a program should be well defined.

In the above, "well-defined" refers to something unambiguous that can be defined and interpreted uniquely.

Obviously, programs directly depend on the programming language used, i.e., commands and operations provided by the language. But there are some common operations defined in all programming languages (with minor changes in styles and programming rules, i.e., *syntax*). These can be categorized as follows:
- Basic algebraic operations, e.g., addition, subtraction, multiplication, and division.
- Equality, assign, and inequality (in conditional statements).
- Some special operations, e.g., absolute value, floor/ceil, powers.
- Boolean operations, e.g., and, or.
- Input/output operations, e.g., read, write, print, return, list, plot.
- Loop statements, e.g., for, while, do.
- Conditional statements, e.g., if, else.
- Termination statements, e.g., end, stop.

In addition to various operations, programming languages provide many built-in functions that can be used to implement algorithms and write programs.

1.4   Programming in R Using Functions

In this book, all programs are written by using the R language, which is freely available at

http://www.r-project.org/

This website also includes manuals and many notes on using R. Note that this book is not an R guide; but we use this flexible language as a tool to implement algorithms and to employ the resulting programs effectively for solving problems. All programs investigated in this book can easily be rewritten by using other programming languages since the underlying algorithms remain the same.

We write programs as *functions* in R. This is because functions perfectly fit into the aims of programming, especially for writing reusable codes. A function in R has the following structure:

```
function_name = function(input1_name,input2_name,...){
    some operations
    some more operations
    return(output_name)
}
```

In the above, the names of the function (`function_name`), inputs (`input1_name`, etc.), and output (`output_name`) are selected by the programmer. Each function is written for a specific purpose to be performed by various operations. These operations produce the output, which is finally extracted from the function using `return` or any other output statement.

Once a function is written in the R editor, it can be saved with the name

```
function_name.R
```

to be used later. In order to use the function, we need to identify it in the R workspace as

```
source("function_name.R")
```

after the working directory is set to the one where the file exists. Then, the function can be executed simply by writing its name with appropriate inputs as

```
myoutput_name = function_name(myinput1_name,myinput2_name,...)
```

which stores the output in `myoutput_name`. Calling the function as

```
function_name(myinput1_name,myinput2_name,...)
```

also works, where the output is printed out rather than stored.

A function can be interpreted as a closed box where inputs are entering and outputs are leaving. Users interact with a function only through inputs and outputs. Therefore, constants and variables used inside a function are not defined outside. Similarly, input and output names, e.g., `input1_name`, `input2_name`, and `output_name` above, are considered to be defined inside the function, and they are not available with the same names outside. This is the reason why we use `myinput1_name`, `myinput2_name`, and `myoutput_name` above to distinguish them from those used in the function.

The next subsection presents some examples that can be considered as warm-up routines before writing and investigating more complicated functions in the next chapters.

1.4.1   Working with Conditional Statements

Let us write a simple program that gives the letter "a" if the input is 1 and the letter "b" if the input is 2. Let the name of the program be `giveletter`. We can use conditional statements to handle different cases.

```
R Program: Print Some Letters (Original)

01 giveletter = function(thenumber){
02    if (thenumber == 1){
03       theletter = "a"
04    }
05    if (thenumber == 2){
06       theletter = "b"
07    }
08    return(theletter)
09 }
```

After writing and saving the program above as giveletter.R, we can identify it as

```
source("giveletter.R")
```

and use it as

```
giveletter(2)
```

that prints out "b" since the input is 2.

In the program above, `theletter` is the output, which is defined only inside the function. For example, if one writes `theletter` in the workspace, R should give an error (if it is not also defined outside by mistake). Similarly, the input `thenumber` is defined only inside the function. In order to use the program, one can also write

```
mynumber = 2
giveletter(mynumber)
```

where `mynumber` is defined outside the function. Moreover, using

```
mynumber = 2
myletter = giveletter(mynumber)
```

stores the result "b" in `myletter`, which is also defined outside the function. In this context, `mynumber` and `myletter` can be considered as variables of the R workspace, even though they are used for input/output.

Computer programs are often restricted to a range of inputs. For example, the program above do not return an output if the input is 3. It may not be fair to expect from programmers to consider all cases (including user mistakes), but sometimes, such a limitation can be considered as a poor programming. Along this direction, the program above can easily be improved by handling "other" cases as follows.

```
R Program: Print Some Letters (Revised)

01 giveletter = function(thenumber){
02     if (thenumber == 1){
03         theletter = "a"
04     }
05     else if (thenumber == 2){
06         theletter = "b"
07     }
08     else{
09         theletter = " "
10     }
11     return(theletter)
12 }
```

The revised program returns the space character if the input is neither 1 nor 2. Note that, in such a case, the original program gives an error and does not produce any useful feedback to the user. If the input is not a number (as a mistake), the revised program also gives an error, which may further be handled with additional checks in the program, if desired. Obviously, for any program, there is a tradeoff between the applicability and simplicity that must be considered carefully by the programmer.

Once a function is written, it can also be used inside another function, provided that it is defined in the R workspace. This increases the reusability of functions and creates a flexible implementation environment, where complicated functions are constructed by using more basic functions. Note that the R language has also many built-in functions that can be used easily when writing programs.

1.5 Some Conventions

Finally, we list some mathematical conventions that are used throughout this book with the corresponding syntax in R.

$A \in R^{m \times n}$ represents a *matrix* involving a total of $m \times n$ real numbers arranged in m rows and n columns. For example,

$$\begin{bmatrix} 1 & 2 & 3 \\ 4 & 5 & 6 \\ 7 & 8 & 9 \end{bmatrix}$$

is a 3×3 matrix involving nine elements. This matrix can be defined in R as

```
A = matrix(c(1,4,7,2,5,8,3,6,9),nrow=3,ncol=3)
```

Here, c(1,4,7,2,5,8,3,6,9) defines an array of numbers in R. This array is used to construct the matrix, where the numbers are arranged columnwise. Sometimes, it may be easier to arrange numbers rowwise, e.g., by using

```
A = matrix(c(1,2,3,4,5,6,7,8,9),nrow=3,ncol=3,"byrow"="true")
```

that produces the same matrix in R.

If a matrix has only one column, it is called a *vector*, e.g., $v \in R^n$ represents a vector of n elements. For example,

$$\begin{bmatrix} 1 \\ 4 \\ 7 \end{bmatrix}$$

is a vector of three elements, which can be defined in R as

```
v = matrix(c(1,4,7),nrow=3,ncol=1)
```

In mathematical point of view, we always consider column vectors (elements arranged as columns) rather than row vectors. If a vector has only one element, i.e., if it is just a single number, we simply call it a *scalar*.

The R language provides a great flexibility in defining vectors and matrices. For example,

```
v = matrix(c(1,4,7,10),ncol=1)
```

defines a vector of four elements, whereas

```
v = matrix(c(1,4,7,10),nrow=16)
```

defines a vector of 16 elements with 1, 4, 7, and 10 are repeated four times. Similarly,

```
A = matrix(0,nrow=16,ncol=16)
```

defines a 16×16 matrix involving a total of 256 zeros.

Let A be an $m \times n$ matrix. Then, $A[m, n]$ represents its element located at the mth row and nth column. We can also define a submatrix B by selecting some rows and columns of A as

$$B = A[k_1 : k_2, l_1 : l_2].$$

Specifically, the matrix B above contains rows of A from k_1 to k_2 and columns of A from l_1 to l_2. Selecting $k_2 = k_1 = k$, we have

$$B = A[k_1 : k_1, l_1 : l_2] = A[k, l_1 : l_2],$$

where B is a row vector involving $l_2 - l_1 + 1$ elements from the kth row of A. Similarly, selecting $l_2 = l_1 = l$ leads to

$$B = A[k_1 : k_2, l_1 : l_1] = A[k_1 : k_2, l],$$

where B is a column vector involving $k_2 - k_1 + 1$ elements from the lth column of A. In R, elements of matrices are accessed and used similar to the mathematical expressions above. For example,

```
B = A[k1:k2,l1:l2]
```

means that some rows and columns of a matrix A are selected and stored in another matrix B.

1.6 Conclusions

Computer programs are written for solving problems on computers. Each program has input(s) and output(s) and is based on an algorithm that describes the procedure to attack and solve a given problem. Efficiency and accuracy are two aspects that should be considered carefully when implementing algorithms and writing programs. In addition to inputs and outputs, programs often contain constants and variables that are not visible to users. Each of these items (inputs, outputs, constants, and variables) can be a scalar, vector, or matrix.

In the next chapters, we will consider R programs written as functions to solve various practical problems. In addition to correct versions, we will investigate incorrect and poor programs that contain possible mistakes and limitations to be avoided along the direction of good programming.

1.7 Exercises

1. Do the following list of operations in the R workspace:

```
i = 5
j = 6
k = i + j
print(k)
j = j + 2
k = k + j
print(k)
k = k*k
print(k)
```

Observe how the value of k (via outputs of the print statements) changes.

2. Write the following program, which finds and returns the larger one of two given numbers:

```
R Program: Find and Print the Larger Number (Original)

01 givelarger = function(i,j){
02     if (i > j){
03         thelarger = i
04     }
05     else{
06         thelarger = j
07     }
08     return(thelarger)
09 }
```

Test your program (after saving and sourcing it) for various inputs, such as

```
givelarger(3,-4)
```

3. Write the following program, which also finds and returns the larger one of two given numbers:

R Program: Find and Print the Larger Number (Revised)

```
01 givelarger = function(i,j){
02     if (i > j){
03         return(i)
04     }
05     else{
06         return(j)
07     }
08 }
```

Test your program (after saving and sourcing it) for various inputs, such as

```
givelarger(3,-4)
```

4. Write an improved program that finds and returns the larger one of two given numbers. As opposed to the programs in Exercises 2 and 3, the program should print "the numbers are equal" and return nothing if the inputs are equal. Test your program (after saving and sourcing it) for various inputs.

5. Use the built-in function $\texttt{atan}$ of R to compute $\tan^{-1}(-1)$, $\tan^{-1}(0)$, and $\tan^{-1}(1)$.

6. In addition to various built-in functions, the R language has many built-in constants. Do the following list of operations in the R workspace:

```
print(pi)
pi = 3
print(pi)
```

As shown in this example, user variables can overwrite the built-in constants, but this should be avoided. Following the operations above, try

```
rm(pi)
print(pi)
```

and observe that the variable $\texttt{pi}$ is removed so that $\texttt{print(pi)}$ gives again the value of the built-in constant. One can also use "Clear Workspace" in the R menu to remove all user-defined objects.

7. Write the following original program, which returns "a" or "b" depending on the input:

```
R Program: Print Some Letters (Original)

01 giveletter = function(thenumber){
02     if (thenumber == 1){
03         theletter = "a"
04     }
05     if (thenumber == 2){
06         theletter = "b"
07     }
08     return(theletter)
09 }
```

Try the program for an input that leads to an error, e.g.,

$$giveletter(3)$$

Explain why the program does not work for such a case. Consider adding the line

$$theletter = "\ "$$

before the conditional statements. Retry the program and explain how it works.

8. Create a 4×3 matrix in the R workspace as

```
A = matrix(c(1,2,3,4,5,6,7,8,9,10,11,12),nrow=4,"byrow"="true")
```

Then, access to different elements of the matrix as follows:

```
A[1,1:3]
A[1:4,2]
A[3,3]
```

Also, try `A[11]`, `A[20]`, `A[5,4]`, `A[1,1,1]` and explain what happens in each case.

Loops

A *loop* is a sequence of instructions, which are required to be executed more than once on purpose. They are initiated by loop statements (for or while) and terminated by termination statements (simply } or sometimes break). Different kinds of loops can be found in almost all practical programs. In this chapter, we consider writing loops and using them for solving various problems. In addition to correct versions, we focus on possible mistakes when writing and implementing loops. Nested loops are also considered for practical purposes, such as matrix–vector multiplications. Finally, we study the iteration concept, which is based on using loops for achieving a convergence.

2.1 Loop Concept

We first consider simple examples involving basic problems and their solutions using loops.

2.1.1 Example: 1-Norm with For Statement

Consider the calculation of the 1-norm of a given vector $v \in \mathbb{R}^n$, i.e.,

$$\|v\|_1 = \sum_{i=1}^{n} |v[i]|.$$

The vector has n elements. The most trivial algorithm to compute the 1-norm can be described as follows:
- Initialize a sum value as zero.
- Add the absolute value of the first element to the sum value.
- Add the absolute value of the second element (if $n > 2$) to the sum value.
- ...
- Add the absolute value of the last element to the sum value.
- Return the sum value.

Ö. Ergül, *Guide to Programming and Algorithms Using R*,
DOI 10.1007/978-1-4471-5328-3_2,
© Springer-Verlag London 2013

Obviously, there is a repetition (adding the absolute value of an element), which can be expressed as a loop. The following R program can be written along this direction:

```
R Program: Calculation of 1-Norm Using For (Original)
01 onenorm_for = function(v){
02     sumvalue = 0
03     for (i in 1:length(v)){
04         sumvalue = sumvalue + abs(v[i])
05     }
06     return(sumvalue)
07 }
```

In this program, we are simply performing addition operations, which could be written as

```
sumvalue = 0 + abs(v[1]) + abs(v[2]) + abs(v[3]) + ...
```

where abs is a built-in function (command) in R. But, instead of writing all addition operations, we use a for loop. This is because of two major reasons:

- We would like to write a general program, where the input vector v may have different numbers of elements.
- Even if the input size is fixed, we are probably unable to write all summation operations one by one if the number of elements in v is large.

When the for loop is used above, the operations inside the loop, i.e.,

```
sumvalue = sumvalue + abs(v[i])
```

are repeated for n times. This is due to the expression

```
i in 1:length(v)
```

in the for statement, which indicates that the variable i will change from 1 to length(v). Here, length(v) is an R command that gives the number of elements in v. The value of the 1-norm is stored in a scalar variable sumvalue, which is returned whenever the loop finishes. The line

```
sumvalue = 0
```

is required to make sure that this scalar is well defined before starting the loop.

At this stage, lets consider some modifications with possible mistakes. In the following program, the loop is constructed correctly, but sumvalue is not updated in accordance with the 1-norm.

```
R Program: Calculation of 1-Norm Using For (Incorrect)
01 onenorm_for = function(v){
02     sumvalue = 0
03     for (i in 1:length(v)){
04         sumvalue = sumvalue + abs(v[1])
05     }
06     return(sumvalue)
07 }
```

Specifically, instead of adding the absolute values of the elements in v, just the absolute value of the first element is added for n times. Hence, the result (output) is

$$\sum_{i=1}^{n} |v[1]| = n|v[1]|,$$

which is simply n times the absolute value of the first element, rather than the 1-norm of the vector.

An example to a correct but poor programming is as follows:

```
R Program: Calculation of 1-Norm Using For (Restricted)

01 onenorm_for = function(v){
02     sumvalue = 0
03     for (i in 1:10){
04         sumvalue = sumvalue + abs(v[i])
05     }
06     return(sumvalue)
07 }
```

In this case, the loop and update operations are written correctly, but the number of elements is fixed to 10. The programmer may be sure that the number of elements in input vectors to be considered and handled via this program is always 10. But, why not to make it more general without too much effort?

The following correct program is quite similar to the original one, but the number of elements is defined as a variable n:

```
R Program: Calculation of 1-Norm Using For (Correct)

01 onenorm_for = function(v){
02     sumvalue = 0
03     n = length(v)
04     for (i in 1:n){
05         sumvalue = sumvalue + abs(v[i])
06     }
07     return(sumvalue)
08 }
```

In some cases, adding some variables may lead to neater expressions. In the example above, the programmer may find

```
for (i in 1:n){
```

neater than the original expression

```
for (i in 1:length(v)){
```

In addition, in computer programs, it is common to use a variable more than once, and using an extra line n = length(v) may prevent repetitive call of the same function, i.e., length in this case.

The following is another correct version, where the variable sumvalue is initialized as the absolute value of the first element:

```
R Program: Calculation of 1-Norm Using For (Correct)

01 onenorm_for = function(v){
02     sumvalue = abs(v[1])
03     n = length(v)
04     for (i in 2:n){
05         sumvalue = sumvalue + abs(v[i])
06     }
07     return(sumvalue)
08 }
```

Note that the loop is constructed as

$$i \text{ in } 2{:}n$$

instead of

$$i \text{ in } 1{:}n$$

to avoid adding the first element twice. As opposed to the previous examples, this program assumes that the vector has at least two elements, i.e., $n > 1$.

2.1.2   Example: 1-Norm with While Statement

Another program to calculate the 1-norm of a given vector is shown below. Compared to the previous programs, the for loop is replaced with a while loop. Even though a different program is implemented now, the underlying algorithm remains the same, i.e., the 1-norm of a vector is calculated by adding the absolute values of its elements one by one.

```
R Program: Calculation of 1-Norm Using While (Original)

01 onenorm_while = function(v){
02     sumvalue = 0
03     i = 1
04     while (i <= length(v)){
05         sumvalue = sumvalue + abs(v[i])
06         i = i + 1
07     }
08     return(sumvalue)
09 }
```

Note the following specific commands due to the structure of the while statement:
- The variable i is initialized as 1 before the loop.
- In addition to the update of the variable sumvalue, the variable i is incremented inside the loop as i = i + 1.

These are because the `while` statement indicates only a condition for stopping the loop whereas no information is provided for the initialization or incrementation, as opposed to the `for` statement, where all possible values of the variable `i` are clearly defined.

Again, let us consider some modifications with possible mistakes. In the following program, the incrementation `i = i + 1` is performed at an incorrect place:

```
R Program: Calculation of 1-Norm Using While (Incorrect)

01 onenorm_while = function(v){
02     sumvalue = 0
03     i = 1
04     while (i <= length(v)){
05         i = i + 1
06         sumvalue = sumvalue + abs(v[i])
07     }
08     return(sumvalue)
09 }
```

This means that the result (output) is

$$\|v\|_1 = \sum_{i=2}^{n+1} |v[i]|$$

instead of the 1-norm of the vector. This expression is mathematically invalid, whereas the program is not expected to give the correct answer (1-norm of the vector). On the other hand, the behavior of the program is actually unpredictable since the program tries to access to the $(n+1)$th element of a vector of n elements. In our case (using R), this probably leads to a not-a-number (NaN) result, but in practice, it is possible that a junk number in memory is extracted by coincidence leading to an incorrect result at the end.

Another incorrect program, where the incrementation of `i` is forgotten, is as follows:

```
R Program: Calculation of 1-Norm Using While (Incorrect)

01 onenorm_while = function(v){
02     sumvalue = 0
03     i = 1
04     while (i <= length(v)){
05         sumvalue = sumvalue + abs(v[i])
06     }
07     return(sumvalue)
08 }
```

This simple mistake leads to the famous *infinite loop*. Since `i` is not incremented, the condition in the `while` statement is always satisfied. Hence, the program continues infinitely (at least in theory!), adding the absolute value of the first element repetitively. This is a very serious problem.

Consider now the following example, where the initialization of i is forgotten:

```
R Program: Calculation of 1-Norm Using While (Incorrect)
01 onenorm_while = function(v){
02     sumvalue = 0
03     while (i <= length(v)){
04         sumvalue = sumvalue + abs(v[i])
05         i = i + 1
06     }
07     return(sumvalue)
08 }
```

This is again a case where the behavior of the program is unpredictable. The variable i is simply undefined before the while statement; hence, we probably get an error indicating that this variable is not found. But, more dangerously, it is possible that i is actually defined (probably incorrectly) in the R workspace before this program is used. In such a case, one may expect that the program gives an incorrect result or a not-a-number (NaN).

A common mistake in loops is mixing for and while statements, such as the loop in the following incorrect program.

```
R Program: Calculation of 1-Norm Using For (Incorrect)
01 onenorm_for = function(v){
02     sumvalue = 0
03     i = 1
04     for (i in 1:length(v)){
05         sumvalue = sumvalue + abs(v[i])
06         i = i + 1
07     }
08     return(sumvalue)
09 }
```

There are two mistakes in this program. The harmless one is the initialization i = 1, which is actually not required since a for loop is used and this statement already defines the initial value of i. However, the second mistake, i.e.,

$$i = i + 1$$

inside the loop, is very dangerous. This is because the loop variable i that should be controlled by the for statement is modified inside the loop. Luckily, R can handle this by omitting the update inside the loop. But, using some other languages, such a mistake may lead to an erratic behavior that is difficult to control. In general, loop variables should not be modified or used for other purposes, except proper increase or decrease commands in while loops.

Finally, the following is a nice and correct variation, where the vector elements are accessed in a reversed order:

```
R Program: Calculation of 1-Norm Using While (Correct)

01 onenorm_while = function(v){
02    sumvalue = 0
03    i = length(v)
04    while (i >= 1){
05        sumvalue = sumvalue + abs(v[i])
06        i = i - 1
07    }
08    return(sumvalue)
09 }
```

Note how i is initialized and updated inside the loop, whereas the condition of the while statement is constructed accordingly.

2.1.3 Example: Finding the First Zero

Lets assume that we would like to find the location of the first zero element of a vector $v \in \mathbb{R}^n$. First, consider the following program using a for statement:

```
R Program: Finding the First Zero Using For (Original)

01 findzero_for = function(v){
02    for (i in 1:length(v)){
03        if (v[i] == 0){
04            return(i)
05        }
06    }
07 }
```

Similar to the previous examples, the elements of the vector are accessed from 1 to n. But, interestingly, the return statement is placed inside the loop. This is because whenever we find a zero element, we would like to stop (there is no need to go on) and return the index of this element. Note that this condition is checked by the if statement as

$$\text{if } (v[i] == 0)\{$$

while the variable i is changed from 1 to n.

The program above does not return anything if there is no any zero in the vector being considered. Even though printing noting would be a good indication for the absence of a zero, one may desire a kind of warning message to be printed in this special case. In fact, it is quite easy to do this as follows:

```
R Program: Finding the First Zero Using For (Correct)

01 findzero_for = function(v){
02     for (i in 1:length(v)){
03         if (abs(v[i]) == 0){
04             return(i)
05         }
06     }
07     return("Vector does not contain zero element!")
08 }
```

We only added a single line

```
return("Vector does not contain zero element!")
```

just after the end of the loop without any extra condition. This is sufficient because we know that, if there is a zero, the program returns its index and stops immediately at line 04. Hence, line 07 is never executed if there is a zero in the vector. Otherwise (if there is no zero in the vector), the loop ends without any return operation, and line 07 is executed next to print out the desired warning.

The algorithm for finding the first zero can also be implemented using a while statement. Consider the following:

```
R Program: Finding the First Zero Using While (Incorrect)

01 findzero_while = function(v){
02     i = 1
03     while (v[i] != 0){
04         i = i + 1
06     }
07     return(i)
08 }
```

In this program, we start by setting the variable i to 1. Then, it is incremented as

$$i = i + 1$$

while the element being considered, i.e., v[i], is not zero. This also means that the loop stops (hence, i is not incremented any further) whenever the element is zero and the condition

$$v[i] != 0$$

is not satisfied. The final value of i is returned as the index of the first zero element.

The program above looks good, but unfortunately it suffers from a serious problem. When there is no zero element in the input vector v, the loop tries to continue even after the last element is checked. Then, the loop attempts to access to the $(n + 1)$th element of the vector, which leads to an error. This is quite different from printing nothing, and the program above can be considered as incorrect.

As a remedy, one can insert an additional condition to stop the while loop when all elements are considered but no zero is found. In other words, the loop variable i should not be allowed to become larger than length(v) whether the vector contains zero or not. Consider the following updated program:

```
R Program: Finding the First Zero Using While (Incorrect)
01 findzero_while = function(v){
02     i = 1
03     while (v[i] != 0 && i <= length(v)){
04         i = i + 1
06     }
07     return(i)
08 }
```

Note that the combined expression

$$v[i] != 0 \ \&\& \ i <= length(v)$$

means that both two conditions, i.e., v[i] != 0 and i <= length(v), need to be satisfied in order to while loop continues. This program is much better than the previous one since the additional condition in the while statement, i.e.,

$$i <= length(v)$$

stops the loop whenever the value of i exceeds the length of v. Unfortunately, even though it does not give any run-time error, this program is also incorrect. A problem occurs again in the special case, i.e., where there is no zero. Specifically, if there is no zero in the vector v, the value of $(n + 1)$ is returned incorrectly as the index of the first zero element. In fact, the program should return nothing or print a warning message to indicate that no zero is found. Hence, we need to add a conditional statement as follows:

```
R Program: Finding the First Zero Using While (Correct)
01 findzero_while = function(v){
02     i = 1
03     while (v[i] != 0 && i <= length(v)){
04         i = i + 1
05     }
06     if (i <= length(v)){
07         return(i)
08     }
09     else{
10         return("Vector does not contain zero element!")
11     }
12 }
```

The final program above is correct, but it looks more complicated that the corresponding program (including the warning message) using a for loop. In many cases, depending on the problem and algorithm, using for or while might be easier than the other, even though the resulting programs have almost the same efficiency.

2.1.4   Example: Infinity Norm

Consider the calculation of the ∞-norm of a given vector $v \in \mathbb{R}^n$, i.e.,

$$\|v\|_\infty = \max_{1 \leq i \leq n} |v[i]|.$$

As the formula states, the ∞-form of a vector is the maximum of the absolute values of its elements. The following program, which checks the absolute values of all elements one by one using a for loop, is suitable for finding the ∞-norm:

```
R Program: Calculation of Infinity-Norm (Original)

01 infinitynorm = function(v){
02     maxvalue = 0
03     for (i in 1:length(v)){
04         if (abs(v[i]) > maxvalue){
05             maxvalue = abs(v[i])
06         }
07     }
08     return(maxvalue)
09 }
```

In this program, the elements of the vector v is considered from 1 to n. Inside the loop, there is an if statement to compare the absolute value of the element being considered with the variable maxvalue. At any instance, this variable, i.e., maxvalue, stores the largest absolute value of the elements that have been considered so far. Then, if the absolute value of the element being considered is larger than maxvalue, this variable should be updated as

```
maxvalue = abs(v[i])
```

accordingly. A program without a conditional statement, such as the following one, would be incorrect:

```
R Program: Calculation of Infinity-Norm (Incorrect)

01 infinitynorm = function(v){
02     maxvalue = 0
03     for (i in 1:length(v)){
04         maxvalue = abs(v[i])
05     }
06     return(maxvalue)
07 }
```

The program above returns nothing but the absolute value of the last element of the input vector v.

We have seen different programs to calculate two different norms of a given vector. At this stage, the following question may arise: Is there any better way to calculate these norms instead of writing these programs? In fact, the answer is yes. For example, consider the following command for the ∞-norm:

```
max(abs(v))
```

It is just a single line, and there is even no need to put this command in a function format. Alternative, if v is correctly defined as a column vector, using

```
norm(v,"I")
```

also works. These examples show that, before attempting to write any program, it is usually better to check whether the programming language (which is R in our case) already provides the desired function or not. For example, using R, there is a norm function, which can be used as above, not only for the ∞-norm, but also for some other norms in mathematics. In addition to saving time for programming, these built-in functions (programmed by the language developers) are generally more efficient (e.g., faster) than those written by users. Of course, no language can provide all functions required. Hence, in real life, computer programs often involve multiple contributions, where user functions and built-in functions are used together appropriately.

2.2 Nested Loops

There is no limitation in putting a loop inside another loop. In such a nested structure, however, the loop variables should be used very carefully, and they should not be mixed. In addition, one should keep in mind that nested loops can be computationally expensive, while they may be implemented if no alternative exists.

2.2.1 Example: Matrix–Vector Multiplication

Consider the multiplication of a matrix $A \in \mathbb{R}^{m \times n}$ with a vector $x \in \mathbb{R}^n$. If $y = Ax$, we have

$$y[i] = \sum_{j=1}^{n} A[i, j]x[j]$$

for $i = 1, 2, \ldots, m$. Hence, a code segment to obtain an element of y can be

```
sumvalue = 0
n = ncol(A)
for (j in 1:n){
    sumvalue = sumvalue + A[i,j]*x[j]
}
y[i] = sumvalue
```

In this code, the command n = ncol(A) gives the number of columns in the input matrix A. We set the value of the variable sumvalue to 0 and update it inside the loop by adding the multiplication of a matrix element with the corresponding element of the input vector x. When the loop finishes, the final value of sumvalue is stored in y. Note that the variable i, which corresponds to the index of the output vector, is assumed to be constant at this stage.

The code segment above should be repeated for all elements of the output vector y, i.e., for different values of i. Therefore, we need this loop to be placed inside another loop as shown in the following program:

```
R Program: Matrix–Vector Multiplication (Original)

01 matvecmult = function(A,x){
02     m = nrow(A)
03     n = ncol(A)
04     y = matrix(0,nrow=m)
05     for (i in 1:m){
06         sumvalue = 0
07         for (j in 1:n){
08             sumvalue = sumvalue + A[i,j]*x[j]
09         }
10         y[i] = sumvalue
11     }
12     return(y)
13 }
```

In this program, the command nrow(A) gives the number of rows in the input matrix A. This value is stored in the variable m, similar to the number of columns that is stored in n. Note that different variables, i.e., i and j, are used for the outer and inner loops, respectively.

In the program above, the variable sumvalue is reinitialized as zero before each inner loop. Having said this, the following program is incorrect:

```
R Program: Matrix–Vector Multiplication (Incorrect)

01 matvecmult = function(A,x){
02     m = nrow(A)
03     n = ncol(A)
04     y = matrix(0,nrow=m)
05     sumvalue = 0
06     for (i in 1:m){
07         for (j in 1:n){
08             sumvalue = sumvalue + A[i,j]*x[j]
09         }
10         y[i] = sumvalue
11     }
12     return(y)
13 }
```

Using this program, where sumvalue is initialized only once outside the loops, only the first element of y can be calculated correctly. Then, the variable sumvalue contains accumulated contributions from earlier calculations leading to incorrect values in the other elements, i.e., from y[2] to y[m].

When there are nested loops, their order is always an issue to be considered by the programmer. In the original matrix–vector multiplication program, the outer and inner loops are constructed for the rows and columns of the matrix A, respectively. Specifically, the variable of the outer loop i represents the rows of A, whereas the variable of the inner loop j represents its columns. This is called a *rowwise* processing of the matrix, because the matrix is accessed row by row, e.g., first all elements in the first row are considered, second all elements in the second row are considered, etc. A *columnwise* processing is also possible, corresponding to a switch of the outer and inner loops in the program.

The nested loops are best switched when there is no operation between them (i.e., no operation inside the outer loop and outside the inner loop). In the original program, line 05, i.e.,

$$\text{sumvalue = 0}$$

is between two loops. Therefore, before attempting to write a matrix–vector multiplication with the matrix accessed columnwise, we can modify the original algorithm slightly by removing the variable sumvalue:

R Program: Matrix–Vector Multiplication (Correct)

```
01 matvecmult = function(A,x){
02     m = nrow(A)
03     n = ncol(A)
04     y = matrix(0,nrow=m)
05     for (i in 1:m){
06         for (j in 1:n){
07             y[i] = y[i] + A[i,j]*x[j]
08         }
09     }
10     return(y)
11 }
```

This program works correctly since the output vector y is initialized as zero in line 04. Moreover, it is now convenient to switch the loops to obtain a columnwise processing of the input matrix as follows:

R Program: Matrix–Vector Multiplication (Correct)

```
01 matvecmult = function(A,x){
02     m = nrow(A)
03     n = ncol(A)
04     y = matrix(0,nrow=m)
05     for (j in 1:n){
06         for (i in 1:m){
07             y[i] = y[i] + A[i,j]*x[j]
08         }
09     }
10     return(y)
11 }
```

Rowwise Processing   Columnwise Processing

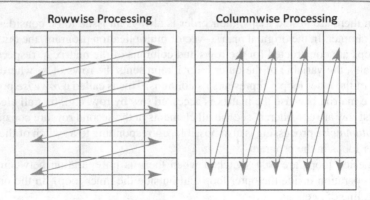

Fig. 2.1 Rowwise and columnwise processing of a matrix

Note how the elements of the matrix A are now used columnwise. As an example, Fig. 2.1 illustrates rowwise and columnwise processing of a 5×5 matrix.

For the matrix–vector multiplication programs demonstrated above, one should also note how the elements of the input and output vectors are used. In the rowwise processing, the input vector x is traced repetitively, whereas the output vector y is traced only once. This is reversed in the columnwise partitioning, where the input vector x is traced once, while the output vector y is traced repetitively.

2.2.2   Example: Closest-Pair Problem

Consider the following problem. Given n points in the two-dimensional space, i.e., (x_k, y_k) for $k = 1, 2, \ldots, n$, find the two closest points. As a *brute-force* approach, where all possible solutions are considered, we can compute the distance between each pair. Then, the minimum of these distances can be selected. We can follow this approach, but instead of storing the distance values between all pairs, we may compute them on-the-fly and compare with a variable minimumdistance, which is simply the minimum distance encountered so far. After considering all possible pairs, this variable and the corresponding index information can be returned as the outputs. Along this direction, the following program can be written:

```
R Program: Finding the Closest Pair (Original)

01 findclosest = function(x,y){
02     n = length(x)
03     minimumdistance = sqrt((x[1]-x[2])^2+(y[1]-y[2])^2)
04     ibackup = 1
05     jbackup = 2
06     for (i in 1:(n-1)){
07         for (j in (i+1):n){
08             distance = sqrt((x[i]-x[j])^2+(y[i]-y[j])^2)
09             if (distance < minimumdistance){
10                 minimumdistance = distance
11                 ibackup = i
12                 jbackup = j
13             }
14         }
15     }
16     list(minimumdistance,ibackup,jbackup)
17 }
```

The inputs of this program are vectors x and y that store the x and y coordinates of the given points, respectively. Both vectors have n elements, where n is stored in a variable n. Initially, the variable minimumdistance is set to the distance between the first and second points as

```
minimumdistance = sqrt((x[1]-x[2])^2+(y[1]-y[2])^2)
```

To keep the track of the pair with the minimum distance, we also use the variables ibackup and jbackup, which are initially set to 1 and 2, respectively. After these initializations, we have two for loops to select different points and to compute the distances between them. In the outer loop, the variable i changes from 1 to $n-1$. In the inner loop, the variable j changes from the value of i+1 to n. This way, all possible pairs are considered without any duplication as the value of i is always smaller than the value of j.

Inside the loops, the distance between the ith and jth points is calculated as

```
distance = sqrt((x[i]-x[j])^2+(y[i]-y[j])^2)
```

This value is then compared with the variable minimumdistance, which stores the minimum distance up to that point. If distance is smaller than minimumdistance, then minimumdistance should be updated accordingly, as well as the indices, i.e.,

```
minimumdistance = distance
ibackup = i
jbackup = j
```

Finally, note that, instead of a return statement, we use

```
list(ibackup,jbackup,minimumdistance)
```

at the end of the program to print out the minimum distance and the indices of the corresponding points.

Fig. 2.2 The closest pair
among 10 points

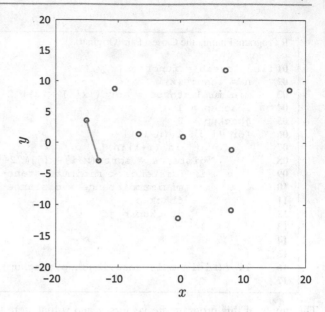

As an example, Fig. 2.2 depicts 10 points on the x–y plane, and the closest pair
found by using the program above.

2.3   Iteration Concept

In a broad sense, an *iterative procedure* is a process of repeating a set of instructions to approach a target. Each repetition is called an *iteration*, and the output of
an iteration is the input of the next iteration. Hence, each iteration depends on all
previous iterations. The aim in performing iterations is to *converge* to a steady state,
but divergence is not uncommon in many iterative solutions.

2.3.1   Example: Number of Terms for e

Assume that we would like to find the number of terms in the expression

$$e = \sum_{i=0}^{\infty} \frac{1}{i!} \approx \sum_{i=0}^{n} \frac{1}{i!}$$

to approximate the value of e with a given error threshold. The following iterative
program can be used for this purpose:

Fig. 2.3 Convergence of the series to the value of *e*

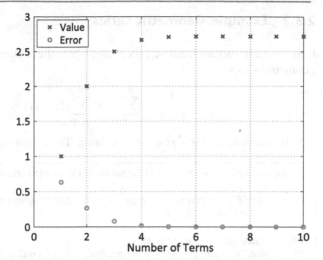

R Program: Finding the Number of Terms for *e* (Original)

```
01 numberoftermsfore = function(desirederror){
02     refvalue = exp(1)
03     term = 1
04     sumvalue = 1 / factorial(term-1)
05     while (abs((refvalue-sumvalue)/refvalue) > desirederror){
06         term = term + 1
07         sumvalue = sumvalue + 1/factorial(term-1)
08     }
09     return(term)
10 }
```

In this program, the variable `term` represents the number of terms used in the series. After this variable is incremented inside the `while` loop, a new term is added into the series as

```
sumvalue = sumvalue + 1/factorial(term-1)
```

where `factorial` is the built-in R function for the factorial. Hence, the variable `sumvalue` is updated in each repetition, and the loop continues while the relative error is larger than the desired value represented by the scalar input `desirederror`. This comparison can be seen in the `while` statement as

```
while (abs((refvalue-sumvalue)/refvalue) > desirederror){
```

where `abs((refvalue-sumvalue)/refvalue)` is the relative error. Note that the reference value is obtained by using the built-in function of R, i.e., `exp(1)`.

Figure 2.3 depicts how the variable `sumvalue` approaches *e*, and the error is reduced to zero as the number of terms increases. In other words, `sumvalue` converges to *e*, whereas the error converges to zero.

2.3.2 Example: Geometric Series

Lets consider another iterative procedure, where the number of terms in the infinite geometric series

$$\frac{1}{1-x} = \sum_{i=0}^{\infty} x^i \approx \sum_{i=0}^{n} x^i, \quad |x| < 1,$$

is to be found again for a given error criteria. The following program can be used:

R Program: Finding the Number of Terms in the Geometric Series (Original)

```
01 numberoftermsingeo = function(x,desirederror){
02     refvalue = 1/(1−x)
03     term = 1
04     sumvalue = x^(term−1)
05     while (abs((refvalue-sumvalue)/refvalue) > desirederror){
06         term = term + 1
07         sumvalue = sumvalue + x^(term−1)
08     }
09     return(term)
10 }
```

In this case, the program has two inputs, i.e., x and desirederror. This program works fine when the variable x, corresponding to the value of x in the formula above, fits into the definition of the geometric series. In other words, a convergence is achieved if the absolute value of the input x is smaller than 1. Otherwise, no convergence occurs, since the geometric series becomes mathematically invalid.

As an example, Fig. 2.4 depicts the variable sumvalue and the corresponding error with respect to the number of terms when the program is used for x equal to 1.01. The value of sumvalue does not converge to any value, whereas the error increases unboundedly as the iterations go on. Hence, in this example, convergence is not achieved, and iterations *diverge*. Note that, for those faulty values of x, the algorithm above never stops (infinite loop occurs), which may be considered as a poor programming.

2.3.3 Example: Babylonian Method

Let us write an iterative program using the Babylonian method, i.e.,

$$x_{n+1} = 0.5(x_n + 5/x_n),$$

to approximate the square root of 5 with 0.001 error. We can start with $x_0 = 2$ and assume that the "exact" value of $\sqrt{5}$ is not available. Hence, we stop iterations when the values in two consecutive iterations are sufficiently close to each other, i.e., $|x_{n+1} - x_n| < 0.001$. The proposed algorithm can be implemented as follows.

Fig. 2.4 Divergence of the geometric series for $x = 1.01$

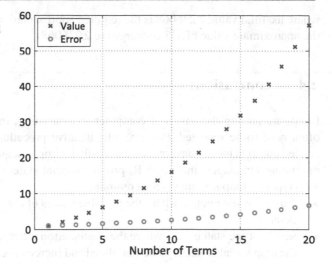

R Program: Babylonian Method for Square-Root of 5 (Original)

```
01 babylonianforsqrtfive = function(){
02    xold = 2
03    xnew = 0.5*(xold + 5/xold)
04    while (abs(xnew-xold) > 0.001){
05        print(xold)
06        xold = xnew
07        xnew = 0.5*(xold + 5/xold)
08    }
09    return(xnew)
10 }
```

This is a quite special program for a specific purpose; there is no input, but the output is the approximate value of $\sqrt{5}$. In addition, the history of iterations is printed out by using `print(xold)` in line 05. There are two variables to keep the values of x. These are the old value `xold` and the new value `xnew`. The variable `xold` is initially set to 2, whereas the variable `xnew` is calculated by using the formula above. The iterative process is constructed by using a `while` statement, which compares the absolute difference of `xold` and `xnew` with the target error 0.001. In the loop, `xold` is updated by simply copying `xnew`, whereas `xnew` is recalculated using the formula again. Note that the order of these updates (first `xold` using `xnew`, then `xnew` using the new value) is important.

If the program above is implemented and used, we get the steps of the iterative procedure in the R workspace as

2
2.25
2.236068

where the final value 2.236068 is the required approximation of $\sqrt{5}$. In other words, the approximate value of $\sqrt{5}$ converges to 2.236068.

2.4   Conclusions

Loops are among the basics of computer programming, in which instructions are often need to be repeated. For example, iterative procedures where iterations are carried out to achieve convergence can easily be implemented using loops. All programming languages, including R, provide special statements to construct loops. Two types of loop statements are common:

- for-type statements, where the possible values of the loop variable are clearly defined.
- while-type statements, where the continuation criteria are clearly defined, but the loop variable needs to be initialized and incremented manually.

Depending on the problem and the solution algorithm, one of the types may be easier to use than the other.

Loops are very beneficial, but they can easily be written incorrectly. Programmers need to check how loops behave under different circumstances, especially to avoid infinite loops, whereas extra conditions may be required to control special cases.

2.5   Exercises

1. Write a program using a for statement to compute the 1-norm of a given vector $v \in \mathbb{R}^n$. Apply the program to an example vector as

```
onenorm_for(matrix(c(4,5,4,3,-1,3,4,5,-4,2),ncol=1))
```

2. Consider the original program for the geometric series. How the program can be changed in order to avoid infinite loop for faulty values of x?

3. Write a program to calculate the 2-norm of a given vector $v \in \mathbb{R}^n$, i.e.,

$$\|v\|_2 = \sqrt{\sum_{i=1}^{n} (v[i])^2},$$

using a for or while loop. Apply it to an example vector as

```
twonorm(matrix(c(5,4,1,6,7,8,-4,15,-2,4),ncol=1))
```

Compare your result with the value given by the built-in function of R, i.e.,

```
norm(matrix(c(5,4,1,6,7,8,-4,15,-2,4),ncol=1),"E")
```

4. Write a program that calculates the sum of cubes of positive integers from 1 to n for a given value of n, i.e.,

$$\sum_{i=1}^{n} i^3.$$

Check your code against the direct formula

$$\sum_{i=1}^{n} i^3 = \left(\frac{n(n+1)}{2} \right)^2$$

for different values of n, such as $n = 3$, $n = 30$, and $n = 300$.

5. Write an R program that counts the number of zeros of a given vector $v \in \mathbb{R}^n$. Apply the program to an example vector as

```
countzeros(matrix(c(4,0,3,0,0,3,-4,0,5,0),ncol=1))
```

6. Write a program that finds the smallest element of a given vector $v \in \mathbb{R}^n$. Apply the program to three different vectors as

```
findminimum(matrix(c(4,0,3,0,0,3,-4,0,5,0),ncol=1))
findminimum(matrix(c(4,2,3,5,6,3,4,1,5,2),ncol=1))
findminimum(matrix(c(-4,-2,-3,-5,-6,-3,-4,-1,-5,-2),ncol=1))
```

Check that your program works correctly with -4, 1, and -6 outputs, respectively.

7. Write a program that finds the two farthest points among n points in the two-dimensional space, i.e., (x_k, y_k) for $k = 1, 2, \ldots, n$. Apply the program to an example problem as

```
x = matrix(c(1,4,3,-2,-3),ncol=1)
y = matrix(c(2,-2,2,2,-1),ncol=1)
findfarthest(x,y)
```

8. Write a program that calculates the sine function using its Taylor-series expansion, i.e.,

$$\sin x = x - \frac{x^3}{3!} + \frac{x^5}{5!} - \frac{x^7}{7!} + \cdots = \sum_{i=0}^{\infty} \frac{(-1)^i x^{2i+1}}{(2i+1)!} \approx \sum_{i=0}^{n} \frac{(-1)^i x^{2i+1}}{(2i+1)!}.$$

The input of the program should be the value of x in terms of radians and the number of added terms n. The output should be the approximate value of $\sin x$. Test your code for $x = \pi/3$ and $n = 1, 2, 3, 4, \ldots$. How many terms are required for six digits of accuracy? Perform similar tests for $x = 4\pi/3$ and $x = 7\pi/2$. Compare your results for different values of x.

Recursions

3

A *recursion* is a repeating process, where a statement is used inside itself. An interesting example to recursion is the experiment when two mirrors are placed parallel to each other so that nested images are formed infinitely. Recursive algorithms are very useful in computer programming, and in many cases, the most efficient program to solve a given problem involves a recursive structure. In this chapter, we again start with simple examples to implement recursions, along with some possible mistakes. Then, we see how recursions can be used effectively to solve more complex problems. Finally, we study a very important concept, namely proof by induction, which is a mathematical tool to analyze and understand recursive expressions.

3.1 Recursion Concept

Efficient or not, most of the programs can be rewritten using a recursion. Nevertheless, we should be very careful when writing recursive programs, particularly when terminating recursions. In programming, we do not want recursions go infinitely.

3.1.1 Example: Recursive Calculation of 1-Norm

Consider again the calculation of the 1-norm of a given vector $v \in \mathbb{R}^n$, i.e.,

$$\|v\|_1 = \sum_{i=1}^{n} |v[i]|.$$

The vector has n elements. A recursive algorithm to compute the 1-norm can be described as follows:

- If the vector has more than one element, divide it into two smaller vectors. Then, the 1-norm of the vector equals the sum of the 1-norms of the smaller vectors.

Ö. Ergül, *Guide to Programming and Algorithms Using R*,
DOI 10.1007/978-1-4471-5328-3_3,
© Springer-Verlag London 2013

- If the vector has only one element, its 1-norm is the absolute value of the element.

The first item defines the recursion. Specifically, computing the 1-norm of a vector requires computing the 1-norms of two smaller vectors. In mathematical point of view, the equality that we are using here is

$$\sum_{i=1}^{n} |v[i]| = \sum_{i=1}^{m} |v[i]| + \sum_{i=m+1}^{n} |v[i]|,$$

where $1 \leq m < n$. This can also be written as

$$\|v\|_1 = \|v[1:m]\|_1 + \|v[m+1:n]\|_1,$$

where the definition of the 1-norm in terms of itself is clearly visible. It should be emphasized that this nice property of the 1-norm allows us to write a recursive algorithm.

The second item in the algorithm above defines how we can terminate the recursion. Any vector with more than one element can be divided into two vectors, but we need to think again whenever we get a vector with only one element. For this special case, we simply have

$$\|v\|_1 = |v[1]|,$$

which means that the 1-norm of the vector is the absolute value of the element.

At this stage, it may be useful to define how to divide a multielement vector into two smaller vectors. A nice selection would be $m \approx n/2$, which can be interpreted as the vector is divided into two vectors of almost equal sizes. It can be shown that this choice leads to the most efficient program, since less recursion steps are required to divide the vector into one-element pieces. On the other hand, we need to consider how to define an approximation to the half of n. For an even n, $m = n/2$ works. For an odd n, however, $m = n/2$ is not meaningful as there is no such a fractional index. To avoid this, one can use $m = \lfloor n/2 \rfloor$, where $\lfloor \cdot \rfloor$ is the floor operation.

Based on the discussions above, we can write the complete formula for our recursion as

$$\|v\|_1 = \begin{cases} \|v[1:m]\|_1 + \|v[m+1:n]\|_1 & \text{for } m = \lfloor n/2 \rfloor & \text{if } n > 1, \\ |v[1]| & & \text{if } n = 1. \end{cases}$$

With the help of this formula, the following R program can be written:

```
R Program: Recursive Calculation of 1-Norm (Original)

01 onenormrecursive = function(v){
02    if (length(v) > 1){
03       sum1 = onenormrecursive(v[1:floor(length(v)/2)])
04       sum2 = onenormrecursive(v[(floor(length(v)/2)+1):length(v)])
05       sumvalue = sum1 + sum2
06    }
07    else{
08       sumvalue = abs(v[1])
09    }
10    return(sumvalue)
11 }
```

Note how an `if` statement is used to distinguish two different cases. For $n > 1$, i.e., when the vector being considered has more than one element, we divide it into two parts, evaluate the 1-norms of these smaller vectors, and then combine these 1-norms to get the 1-norm of the vector. Interestingly, we do not directly compute the 1-norms of the smaller vectors. In fact, we just use the program that we are currently writing! These are performed by three lines as

```
sum1 = onenormrecursive(v[1:floor(length(v)/2)])
sum2 = onenormrecursive(v[(floor(length(v)/2)+1):length(v)])
sumvalue = sum1 + sum2
```

by employing the program `onenormrecursive` in itself. When the vector being considered has only one element, the only line being executed is

```
sumvalue = abs(v[1])
```

as required.

To improve its readability, the recursive program can be rewritten as follows:

```
R Program: Recursive Calculation of 1-Norm (Correct)

01 onenormrecursive = function(v){
02    n=length(v)
03    m=floor(n/2)
04    if (n > 1){
05       sum1 = onenormrecursive(v[1:m])
06       sum2 = onenormrecursive(v[(m+1):n])
07       sumvalue = sum1 + sum2
08    }
09    else{
10       sumvalue = abs(v[1])
11    }
12    return(sumvalue)
13 }
```

In this program, the number of elements and the partitioning point are stored in variables n and m, respectively.

Fig. 3.1 Recursive
calculation of the 1-norm of a
simple vector

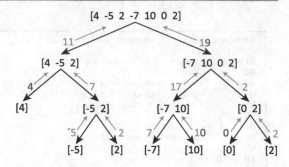

Each person has her/his own way of understanding recursion, but one common
method is to construct a tree structure using simple examples. For the program
above, consider the vector

$$v = [4 \quad -5 \quad 2 \quad -7 \quad 10 \quad 0 \quad -2]$$

involving seven elements. Figure 3.1 depicts a tree structure on how the 1-norm of
this vector is calculated recursively. In this figure, we observe the partitioning of
vectors into smaller vectors until the number of elements is reduced to only one.
Combinations of outputs from bottom to top lead to the final output $11 + 19 = 30$,
which is the 1-norm of v.

The efficiency of a recursive program is often related to the depth of recursion,
which can be defined as the number of levels in a tree structure associated with a
solution using a recursive program. For the recursive calculation of the 1-norm with
equally divided vectors, the depth of recursion is approximately $n/2$ if the initial
vector has n elements.

One of the common confusions in recursive programming is regarding variables.
For example, using the program above, what is the value of n if the program calls
itself and smaller vectors are considered repetitively? A correct answer would be
that n is the number of elements in any vector being considered. As the recursion
continues, multiple n values appear, but they are not mixed since variable values
are locally defined within functions and each call of the function means a new n.
This can be seen easily if a print statement like `print(n)` is placed in the program
above.

Now, let us see some possible mistakes that can be done in writing recursive
programs. Consider the following:

```
R Program: Recursive Calculation of 1-Norm (Incorrect)

01 onenormrecursive = function(v){
02     if (length(v) > 1){
03         sum1 = onenormrecursive(v[1:floor(length(v)/2)])
04         sum2 = onenormrecursive(v[(floor(length(v)/2)+1):length(v)])
05         sumvalue = sum1 + sum2
06     }
07     return(sumvalue)
08 }
```

In this program, the termination condition is forgotten. Therefore, as the recursion continues and whenever a vector with only one element is encountered (note that this eventually happens for any initial vector), the program tries to return `sumvalue`, which is not defined. Therefore, the program stops with an error.

In the following one, there is not even a condition defined:

```
R Program: Recursive Calculation of 1-Norm (Incorrect)

01 onenormrecursive = function(v){
02      sum1 = onenormrecursive(v[1:floor(length(v)/2)])
03      sum2 = onenormrecursive(v[(floor(length(v)/2)+1):length(v)])
04      sumvalue = sum1 + sum2
05   return(sumvalue)
06 }
```

Since there is no condition and termination, one may expect that this program runs infinitely, especially due to the line

```
sum2 = onenormrecursive(v[(floor(length(v)/2)+1):length(v)])
```

To understand what actually happens, consider a vector v with only one element, i.e., $n = 1$. Then, $m = \lfloor n/2 \rfloor = 0$ and $m + 1 = 1$, which means that the program is executed with the same input vector (through line 03) again and again. Luckily, the R environment automatically detects infinite recursions, and the program above stops immediately with an error indicating this particular problem.

The following can be considered as an example to a poor programming:

```
R Program: Recursive Calculation of 1-Norm (Poor)

01 onenormrecursive = function(v){
02      if (length(v) > 1){
03          sum1 = onenormrecursive(v[1:1])
04          sum2 = onenormrecursive(v[2:length(v)])
05          sumvalue = sum1 + sum2
06      }
07      else{
08          sumvalue = abs(v[1])
09      }
10      return(sumvalue)
11 }
```

In this case, the vector considered is not divided equally, but instead, it is divided into a vector of only one element and another vector containing the rest. Hence, vectors are not divided effectively in this program. It can be shown that, using this program, the depth of the recursion is n (rather than $n/2$) if the initial vector has n elements.

3.1.2 Example: Fibonacci Numbers

Fibonacci numbers starting from 1 can be written as

$$1, 1, 2, 3, 5, 8, 13, 21, 34, 55, \ldots,$$

where each number (except for the first two numbers) is the sum of two previous numbers. This recurrence relation can be written as

$$f(i) = f(i-1) + f(i-2), \quad i > 2,$$

with conditions $f(1) = 1$ and $f(2) = 1$. Then, the following recursive program can be written to find the ith Fibonacci number:

R Program: Recursive Calculation of ith Fibonacci Number (Original)

```
01 fiborecursive = function(i){
02     if (i <= 2){
03         value = 1
04     }
05     else{
06         value1 = fiborecursive(i-1)
07         value2 = fiborecursive(i-2)
08         value = value1 + value2
09     }
10     return(value)
11 }
```

The program simply returns 1 if the variable i corresponding to the value of i is smaller than or equal to 2. Otherwise, the program itself is called twice; one for i-1 and the other for i-2. Then, the results of these calls are added together to get the ith Fibonacci number.

In the program above, we do not have to define variables to store intermediate values. Hence, the program can easily be shortened as follows:

R Program: Recursive Calculation of ith Fibonacci Number (Correct)

```
01 fiborecursive = function(i){
02     if (i <= 2){
03         value = 1
04     }
05     else{
06         value = fiborecursive(i-1) + fiborecursive(i-2)
07     }
08     return(value)
09 }
```

On the R side, this program is not very different from the original one. The original three lines are replaced with line 06, i.e.,

```
value = fiborecursive(i-1) + fiborecursive(i-2)
```

When this line is executed, the function is first called for `i-1` and `i-2`. The results of these calls are stored by R, but they are not available as variables to the user. Their summation, however, is assigned to the variable `value`, which is returned as the output of the program.

Many programmers are keen to shorten their programs for practical purposes. As an example, the program above can be further shortened as follows:

R Program: Recursive Calculation of *i*th Fibonacci Number (Correct)

```
01 fiborecursive = function(i){
02     if (i <= 2){
03         return(1)
04     }
05     else{
06         return(fiborecursive(i-1)+fiborecursive(i-2))
07     }
08 }
```

In this case, the sum `fiborecursive(i-1)+fiborecursive(i-2)` is returned without even storing it in any variable. Since the outputting is carried inside the `if` statement, two `return` statements are required for different conditions, even though only one of them is executed depending on the value of the variable `i`. Along this direction, the following program is incorrect and leads to the infinite-recursion error.

R Program: Recursive Calculation of *i*th Fibonacci Number (Incorrect)

```
01 fiborecursive = function(i){
02     return(fiborecursive(i-1)+fiborecursive(i-2))
03 }
```

3.1.3 Example: Factorial

The factorial of a number can easily be calculated using a recursive algorithm. Even though there is a built-in function `factorial` in R, we consider this as a good example of recursion. Writing the factorial operation as

$$i! = i \times (i - 1) \times (i - 2) \times \cdots \times 1,$$

we note the recurrence relation $i! = i \times (i - 1)!$ and the termination condition $0! = 1$, which can be used to write the following program:

```
R Program: Recursive Calculation of Factorial (Original)

01 factorialrecursive = function(i){
02     if (i == 0){
03         value = 1
04     }
05     else{
06         value = i*factorialrecursive(i-1)
07     }
08     return(value)
09 }
```

Similar to the previous examples, this program can be shortened by removing the variable `value` as follows:

```
R Program: Recursive Calculation of Factorial (Correct)

01 factorialrecursive = function(i){
02     if (i == 0){
03         return(1)
04     }
05     else{
06         return(i*factorialrecursive(i-1))
07     }
08 }
```

Note that the multiplication `i*factorialrecursive(i-1))` needs to be performed before the return operation, but this is performed implicitly by R without any intermediate value (variable) available to the user.

3.2   Using Recursion for Solving Problems

Up to this point, we have seen how to construct a recursive approach and write recursive programs to solve a given problem. In this section, we consider some problems, which can be solved most naturally by recursive algorithms.

3.2.1   Example: Highest Common Factor

Let a nonnegative integer (natural number) $i \in \mathbb{N}$ be factorized as $i = a \times b$, where $a, b \in \mathbb{N}$. Both a and b are called factors of i. Each natural number i has a set of factors including at least 1 and itself. Then, the highest common factor (HCF) of a set of natural numbers $\{i_1, i_2, \ldots, i_m\}$ is defined as the largest integer, which is the factor of all numbers in the set.

The highest common factor of two numbers can be obtained by a recursive algorithm, namely, a recursive version of the Euclidean algorithm. The Euclidean algorithm is based on the following observation. If HCF$\{i, j\}$ is the highest common factor of i and j, where $i \geq j$, it is also the highest common factor of $(i - j)$ and j. Note that if $i = a \times \text{HCF}\{i, j\}$ and $j = b \times \text{HCF}\{i, j\}$, then $(i - j) = (a - b) \times \text{HCF}\{i, j\}$.

Based on the discussion above, the following program can be written:

R Program: Finding HCF Using Recursive Euclidean Algorithm (Original)

```
01 hcfeuclidean = function(i,j){
02    if (j == 0){
03        hcfvalue = i
04    }
05    else{
06        k = i %% j
07        hcfvalue = hcfeuclidean(j,k)
08    }
09    return(hcfvalue)
10 }
```

First, assume that the first input $\texttt{i}$ is greater than or equal to the second input $\texttt{j}$. As described above, the smaller integer can be subtracted from the larger integer without changing their HCF. This idea is used in line 06 as

$$\texttt{k = i \%\% j}$$

where the built-in modulus function $\texttt{\%\%}$ is used. Specifically, in this line, the modulus function is used to subtract a multiple of $\texttt{j}$ from $\texttt{i}$. Instead of a single subtraction, the modulus function (corresponding to one or multiple subtractions) is used so that the resulting value $\texttt{k = i \%\% j}$ is always smaller than $\texttt{j}$. This can be interpreted as $\texttt{j}$ is repetitively subtracted from $\texttt{i}$ until a smaller integer is obtained. Then, the program calls itself with the new inputs $\texttt{j}$ and $\texttt{k}$, where the former is the larger integer now.

Interestingly, this program works correctly even when the first input $\texttt{i}$ is smaller than the second input $\texttt{j}$. If this is the case, the modulus operation in line 06 returns $\texttt{i}$ without subtracting anything. Then, the program calls itself (in line 07) as

$$\texttt{hcfvalue = hcfeuclidean(j,i)}$$

where the inputs are switched without any change in their values. In other words, if the first input is smaller, then the program automatically switches the inputs in the first call of the recursion.

In the program above, the recursion is controlled by an $\texttt{if}$ statement. In any call of this program, if the smaller integer is zero, then the output is the other integer (see line 03). Note that, as a recursion continues and integers are subtracted from each other, this condition occurs eventually, leading to the termination of the recursion.

3.2.2 Example: Lowest Common Multiple

The lowest common multiple (LCM) of two positive integers i and j is defined as the smallest integer that is the multiple of both i and j. In other words, $\text{LCM}\{i, j\} = a \times i$ and $\text{LCM}\{i, j\} = b \times j$ such that a and b are the smallest possible integers.

The lowest common multiple of two numbers is related to their highest common factor as

$$\text{LCM}\{i, j\} = \frac{i \times j}{\text{HCF}\{i, j\}}.$$

Hence, the following program can be used to easily find the lowest common multiple. Even though it involves a single command (other than the function definition and the `return` line), we write it as a function to use later:

```
R Program: Finding LCM Using HCF (Original)

01 lcmusinghcf = function(i,j){
02     lcmvalue = i*j / hcfeuclidean(i,j)
03     return(lcmvalue)
04 }
```

Now, let us consider the lowest common multiple of a set of positive integers $\{i_1, i_2, \ldots, i_n\}$. We note that

$$\text{LCM}\{i_1, i_2, \ldots, i_n\} = \text{LCM}\{i_1, \text{LCM}\{i_2, \ldots, i_n\}\}.$$

In other words, the lowest common multiple can be defined recursively using itself. The following program can be written following this strategy:

```
R Program: Finding LCM of a Vector of Numbers (Original)

01 lcmvector = function(v){
02     n = length(v)
03     if (n == 2){
04         lcmvalue = lcmusinghcf(v[1],v[2])
05     }
06     else{
07         j = lcmvector(v[2:n])
08         lcmvalue = lcmusinghcf(v[1],j)
09     }
10     return(lcmvalue)
11 }
```

The input of this program is a vector v that contains positive integers whose lowest common multiple is to be found. If there are only two elements in this vector, the program `lcmusinghcf` is called directly using these elements, i.e., v[1] and v[2], in line 04. This (having two elements) is also the termination case of the recursion. For more than two elements, lines 07 and 08 are performed, which can be described as follows.

• Line 07: Find the lowest common multiple of elements from v[2] to v[n]. This is where the program calls itself.

Fig. 3.2 Towers of Hanoi involving four disks

- Line 08: The output (the lowest common multiple of all elements) is the lowest common multiple of the first element and the result of line 07. The program `lcmusinghcf` can be used here since there are only two numbers (the first element and the result of line 07).

Note how a recursive program `lcmvector` uses another recursive program `hcfeuclidean` with an interface `lcmusinghcf` between them. In computer science, implementations usually involve multiple programs and code segments interacting with each other, as in this particular case.

3.2.3 Example: Towers of Hanoi

A very famous set of problems that can be solved recursively is Towers of Hanoi. As depicted in Fig. 3.2, the puzzle involves three rods and a given number of (originally eight but four in this example) disks that can slide on the rods. Initially, the disks are stacked in one of the rods (source rod on the left) based on their sizes, i.e., from the smallest on the top to the largest on the bottom leading to a conical shape. The aim is to transfer the entire stack to another rod (destination rod on the right), again resulting in a conical shape. There is also a buffer rod in the middle to facilitate the movements. The rules are as follows:

- Only one disk may be moved at a time.
- Each move involves taking a disk on the top of a stack and putting it on the top of another stack.
- A disk cannot be placed on a smaller disk.

A particular aim is to perform the transfer of the stack with a minimum number of movements.

Initially, the solution of the puzzle may not seem trivial, but in fact, it is easy using a recursive approach. Consider the version depicted in Fig. 3.2 involving four disks. The following observations can be made:

- For the solution of the problem, the largest disk on the source (left) rod is eventually moved to the destination (right) rod.
- In order to perform this movement, other three disks should reside on the buffer (middle) rod with a conical shape. Specifically, this is the only scenario that such a movement can be done based on the given rules.
- Then, the solution of the original problem involves the solution of a similar (smaller) problem, where the smaller three rods are transferred from the source (left) rod to the buffer (middle) rod and then, from the buffer (middle) rod to the destination (left) rod.

Obviously, the items above describe a recursive process. In order to solve the problem involving four disks, we need to solve a subproblem involving three disks twice. Similarly, the solution of a three-disk problem requires the solution of a smaller problem involving only two disks. Now, lets write all operations one by one and construct the recursive structure.

- Solution for four disks (transfer from a source to a destination):
  - – Step 1: Move the smaller three disks from the source rod to the buffer rod. (Perform the solution of this subproblem as described below.)
  - – Step 2: Move the largest disk (among four disks) to the destination rod.
  - – Step 3: Move the smaller three disks from the buffer rod to the destination rod. (Perform the solution of this subproblem as described below.)
- Solution for three disks (transfer from a source to a destination):
  - – Step 1: Move the smaller two disks from the source rod to the buffer rod. (Perform the solution of this subproblem as described below.)
  - – Step 2: Move the largest disk (among three disks) to the destination rod.
  - – Step 3: Move the smaller two disks from the buffer rod to the destination rod. (Perform the solution of this subproblem as described below.)
- Solution for two disks (transfer from a source to a destination):
  - – Step 1: Move the smaller disk from the source rod to the buffer rod.
  - – Step 2: Move the larger disk to the destination rod.
  - – Step 3: Move the smaller disk from the buffer rod to the destination rod.

In the solutions described above, the terms "source", "buffer", and "destination" are redefined for each problem. In other words, each problem and its solution always involve a transfer of rods from the source rod to the destination rod while using the buffer rod. Hence, one need to be very careful when calling the recursive function since, for example, the buffer rod for the parent problem can be the source rod or destination rod for the subproblem.

A pseudocode for the solution of Towers of Hanoi with arbitrary numbers of disks can be written as follows:

```
Pseudocode: Solution of Towers of Hanoi

01 towersofhanoi = function(n,sourcerod,bufferrod,destinationrod){
02     if (n == 0){
03         do nothing
04     }
05     else{
06         towersofhanoi(n-1,sourcerod,destinationrod,bufferrod)
07         move from sourcerod to destinationrod
06         towersofhanoi(n-1,bufferrod,sourcerod,destinationrod)
08     }
10 }
```

The orders of the rods in the recursive calls should be particularly noted, in accordance with the discussion above.

Figure 3.3 depicts the solution of a four-disk problem, which requires a total of 15 movements. At this stage, we can find the minimum number of movements required to solve any given number of disks. This way, we can set the optimality criteria before solving the problem for large numbers of disks.

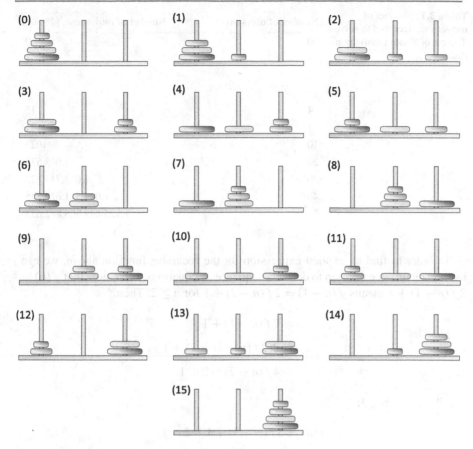

Fig. 3.3 The solution of Towers of Hanoi involving four disks

Consider the solution of Towers of Hanoi with n disks. As detailed above, such a solution requires two smaller solutions involving $n-1$ disks, in addition to a movement of the largest disk. Hence, one can write

$$f(n) = 2f(n-1) + 1,$$

where f represents the number of movements. Unsurprisingly, the number of movements is a recursive function, i.e., a function defined by using itself. In fact, recursive programs and algorithms often have recursive costs (here the number of movements can be interpreted as the cost). For the termination of the recurrence relation, one can also add $f(0) = 0$, so that $f(1) = 1$ is the number of movements for the trivial one-disk problem.

Table 3.1 Number of
movements required to solve
Towers of Hanoi involving n
disks

Number of disks (n)	Number of movements ($2^n - 1$)
0	0
1	1
2	3
3	7
4	15
5	31
10	1023
20	1,048,575
30	1,073,741,823
40	1,099,511,627,775
50	1,125,899,906,842,623

In order to find an explicit expression for the recursive function above, we can use the recurrence relation to derive a sequence of equations. First, note that $f(n) = 2f(n-1) + 1$ means $f(n-1) = 2f(n-2) + 1$ for $n \geq 2$. Then,

$$\begin{aligned} f(n) &= 2f(n-1) + 1 \\ &= 2(2f(n-2) + 1) + 1 \\ &= 4f(n-2) + 2 + 1. \end{aligned}$$

Similarly, for $n \geq 3$,

$$f(n) = 8f(n-3) + 4 + 2 + 1.$$

It appears that, considering an arbitrarily large n, we have

$$f(n) = 2^{n-1} f(1) + 2^{n-2} + \cdots + 8 + 4 + 2 + 1,$$

which can be rewritten as

$$f(n) = 2^{n-1} + 2^{n-2} + \cdots + 8 + 4 + 2 + 1 = \sum_{i=0}^{n-1} 2^i$$

since $f(1) = 1$. Evaluating the summation, we get

$$f(n) = \sum_{i=0}^{n-1} 2^i = \frac{1 - 2^n}{1 - 2} = 2^n - 1$$

as the explicit expression, which is valid for all values of $n \geq 0$.

Table 3.1 lists the number of movements to solve Towers of Hanoi with respect to the number of disks n.

Fig. 3.4 Recursive
binary-search algorithm
applied to a simple vector

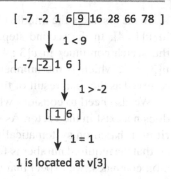

Obviously, the number of movements grows rapidly (exponentially to be more specific). To formally prove that $f(n) = 2^n - 1$ is the direct formula for the recursion $f(n) = 2f(n-1) + 1$, we need *proof by induction*, which is considered in the last section of this chapter.

3.2.4 Example: Binary Search

Consider a recursive binary-search algorithm, which finds the position of a given number in a vector $v \in \mathbb{R}^n$ involving sorted numbers:

- Take the vector, as well as a lower index and a higher index. The number is to be searched between these lower and higher indices.
- Take the number in the middle of the range between the lower and higher indices. If it is the one that we are looking for, then the algorithm stops by returning its index.
- If the number that we are searching is smaller than the middle element, the algorithm is restarted by considering the smaller elements (from the lower index to the middle index, excluding the middle index).
- If the number that we are searching is larger than the middle element, the algorithm is restarted by considering the larger elements (from the middle index to the higher index, excluding the middle index).

This is called a recursive binary-search algorithm, since it is based on recursively dividing the vector into *two* smaller vectors until the number is found. It is of course possible to find the searched element by scanning all elements of the given vector, but the binary-search algorithm is much more efficient than a direct scan, as discussed in Chap. 4.

As an example, consider a simple vector of nine elements

$$v = [-7, -2, 1, 6, 9, 16, 28, 66, 78]$$

and assume that we are searching the number 1 (located at $v[3]$) in it. Note that, as an important requirement for the proposed algorithm working correctly, the numbers in the vector are sorted in the ascending order. Figure 3.4 depicts a tree structure on how the number is searched and found.

In the first step, the middle element is $v[5] = 9$. Since $1 < 9$, the search continues in $v[1 : 4]$. In the second step, the middle element is $v[2] = -2$. Since $1 > -2$, the search continues in $v[3 : 4]$. In the third and final step, the middle element is $v[3] = 1$, which is the number that we are searching. Hence, its index, i.e., 3, is returned as the final result of the search.

We also need to consider what happens when the number that we are searching does not exist in the vector. As shown in the example above, the binary-search algorithm is based on systematically limiting the range of elements that we are looking so that the required number is found after a number of steps. Therefore, as the recursion continues, we expect that the lower and higher indices approach to each other. If, at some step, the higher index is smaller than the lower index, it can be claimed that the number is not found and the algorithm must stop.

Considering the discussion above, the following program can be written. The inputs of this program are the vector v, the number that we are searching thenumber, and lower/higher indices of the search lowerindex and higherindex. In the initial call of this program, lowerindex is set to 1, while higherindex is set to n to consider all elements of the vector.

```
R Program: Recursive Binary Search (Original)

01 binarysearchrecursive = function(v,thenumber,lowerindex,higherindex){
02    if (lowerindex > higherindex){
03       print("The number is not found!")
04    }
05    else{
06       middleindex = lowerindex + floor((higherindex-lowerindex)/2)
07       if (v[middleindex] == thenumber){
08          return(middleindex)
09       }
10       else if (v[middleindex] < thenumber){
11          binarysearchrecursive(v,thenumber,middleindex+1,higherindex)
12       }
13       else if (v[middleindex] > thenumber){
14          binarysearchrecursive(v,thenumber,lowerindex,middleindex-1)
15       }
16    }
17 }
```

The program starts with an if statement to compare lowerindex and higherindex. If lowerindex is larger than higherindex, then the program stops and prints a warning message to indicate that the number is not found in the vector; this is the termination point of the recursion. Otherwise, the program may continue. The variable middleindex is calculated in line 06 as

```
middleindex = lowerindex + floor((higherindex-lowerindex)/2)
```

which is followed by the comparison of the middle element v[middleindex] with the number to be found, i.e., thenumber. The program returns middleindex, if the equality in line 07 holds. Otherwise, the program itself is called with a new search range that is determined according to the value of v[middleindex] with respect to thenumber.

3.2.5 Example: Sequence Generation

Assume that we would like to list all words with n letters. For simplicity, these words contain only "a" and "b", but we would like to find all possible combinations whether the word is meaningful or not. The following recursive algorithm can be used for this purpose:

- Put "a" as the first letter. Then, solve the problem for $n - 1$ letters if $n > 1$ and add the result next to "a".
- Put "b" as the first letter. Then, solve the problem for $n - 1$ letters if $n > 1$ and add the result next to "b".
- Combine the two items above for the complete list.

Obviously, the solution of the problem (listing words) for n letters depends on the solution of the problem (listing words) for $n - 1$ letters. Hence, this is a recursive algorithm.

In order to write the recursive program, we use two combination operations, i.e., rbind for rowwise combinations and cbind for columnwise combinations. Results are stored as matrices. For n letters, we expect 2^n different words. As an example, if $n = 3$, the words to be listed are "aaa", "aab", "aba", "abb", "baa", "bab", "bba", and "bbb", which can be written as a matrix, i.e.,

$$\begin{bmatrix} a & a & a \\ a & a & b \\ a & b & a \\ a & b & b \\ b & a & a \\ b & a & b \\ b & b & a \\ b & b & b \end{bmatrix}.$$

The proposed recursive algorithm described above can be implemented shortly as follows:

```
R Program: Generate Words With a and b (Original)

01 generateab = function(n){
02     if (n > 0){
03         v = rbind(matrix("a",nrow=2^(n-1)),matrix("b",nrow=2^(n-1)))
04         return(noquote(cbind(v,rbind(generateab(n-1),generateab(n-1)))))
05     }
06 }
```

The program above is very compact and it contains few lines, but each line should be investigated carefully to understand how such a program generates and prints all words with n letters.

First, lets focus on line 03. This line initializes a vector v with 2^n elements. The first half of these elements are the character "a", whereas the second half are the character "b". Note that the commands

```
matrix("a",nrow=2^(n-1))
```

and

$$\text{matrix("b",nrow=2}^{\wedge}\text{(n-1))}$$

generate vectors of 2^{n-1} elements, which are then combined using rbind and stored in v. As an example, if $n = 3$, one can expect that v contains

$$\begin{bmatrix} a \\ a \\ a \\ a \\ b \\ b \\ b \\ b \end{bmatrix}.$$

In line 04, the function itself is called twice with an input of n-1, i.e.,

$$\text{generateab(n-1)}$$

We expect that the results of these calls are identical matrices involving 2^{n-1} rows and $n - 1$ columns containing the solution for the input $n - 1$. These matrices are combined using rbind as

$$\text{rbind(generateab(n-1),generateab(n-1))}$$

leading to a matrix with 2^n rows. As an example, if $n = 3$, rbind above is expected to create the matrix

$$\begin{bmatrix} a & a \\ a & b \\ b & a \\ b & b \\ a & a \\ a & b \\ b & a \\ b & b \end{bmatrix}.$$

Finally, the result of rbind is combined columnwise with v (prepared as discussed above) as

$$\text{cbind(v,rbind(generateab(n-1),generateab(n-1)))}$$

which is the desired output to be returned. Before returning, we use the built-in noquote command to omit quotation marks in the output.

In the program above, the if statement is particularly important to terminate the recursion appropriately. For any input $n > 1$, the program calls itself with smaller inputs. When $n = 1$, line 03 generates a vector of two elements containing "a" and "b". At this stage, there is nothing to add after these letters; therefore, the calls with a smaller input ($n = 0$) should return nothing. This is precisely controlled by the if statement in line 02, which guarantees that the program neither calls itself nor returns anything when $n = 0$.

One way to improve the program above is storing the result of generateab(n-1)) and using it twice, rather than calling the function twice. This does not change

Fig. 3.5 Producing A_{1j} from A for the calculation of the determinant

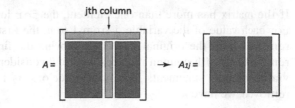

the depth of recursion (that is n) but improves the efficiency by reducing the number of function calls.

3.2.6 Example: Determinant

Determinant is an important quantity for square matrices, and there are various ways, including a recursive approach, to calculate this quantity. Using a recursive approach, the determinant of an arbitrary square matrix $A \in \mathbb{R}^{n \times n}$ can be written as

$$\det(A) = A[1,1] \det(A_{11}) + \cdots + A[1,j](-1)^{1+j} \det(A_{1j})$$
$$+ \cdots + A[1,n](-1)^{1+n} \det(A_{1n}),$$

where A_{1j} represent an $(n-1) \times (n-1)$ matrix obtained by deleting the first row and the jth column of A. Figure 3.5 presents an illustration of producing A_{1j} from A.

The recursive formula above is valid when $n > 1$. For $n = 1$, $\det(A) = A[1,1]$, i.e., the determinant is simply the value of the single element. Based on the recurrence relation and the termination condition, the following program can be written:

```
R Program: Recursive Calculation of Determinant (Original)

01 determinantrecursive = function(A){
02     n = nrow(A)
03     if (n == 1){
04         value = A[1,1]
05     }
06     else{
07         value = 0
08         for (j in (1:n)){
09             if (j == 1){
10                 A1j = matrix(A[2:n,2:n],nrow=n-1)
11             }
12             else if (j == n){
13                 A1j = matrix(A[2:n,1:(n-1)],nrow=n-1)
14             }
15             else{
16                 A1j = cbind(A[2:n,1:(j-1)],A[2:n,(j+1):n])
17             }
18             value1 = determinantrecursive(A1j)
19             value2 = A[1,j]*(-1)^(j+1)
20             value = value + value1*value2
21         }
22     }
23     return(value)
24 }
```

If the matrix has more than one element, the `for` loop (lines 08–21) is executed. For each value of the variable j from 1 to n, the first row and the jth column are removed from the original matrix. Removing the first row is relatively easy, but removing the jth column requires a careful consideration of three different cases via conditional statements. When the value of j is 1 and the first column is to be removed, we have

```
A1j = matrix(A[2:n,2:n],nrow=n-1)
```

where the column index is `2:n` to indicate that the columns of A from 2 to n are selected. Similarly, when the value of j is n and the last column is to be removed, we have

```
A1j = matrix(A[2:n,1:(n-1)],nrow=n-1)
```

where the column index is now `1:(n-1)`. For all other values of j from 2 to $n-1$, removing the jth column requires the selection of two submatrices, i.e., `A[2:n,1:(j-1)]` and `A[2:n,(j+1):n]`, and then their columnwise combination as

```
A1j = cbind(A[2:n,1:(j-1)],A[2:n,(j+1):n])
```

Whenever the submatrix A1j is obtained, its determinant is calculated by using the program itself as

```
value1 = determinantrecursive(A1j)
```

which is multiplied with

```
value2 = A[1,j]*(-1)^(j+1)
```

in accordance with the formula of the determinant. The multiplication is then added to the output `value`, which is returned after all j values are considered.

Even though the program above is relatively simple compared to some other methods for calculating the determinant, it is very expensive. Specifically, its time complexity is $\mathcal{O}(n!)$, where n represents the size of the matrix. Therefore, the determinant of a matrix is usually calculated with more efficient methods, such as the LU factorization, especially when the matrix is large. Nevertheless, the procedure above is a good example on the application of a recursive algorithm to solve a practical problem.

3.3   Proof by Induction

Proof by induction is a powerful tool in mathematics to prove various statements, including recurrence relations. In many cases, recursive formulas need to be converted into direct formulas, which can be performed heuristically and then, proven via induction. An induction is based on two simple rules:
(1)   Show that the statement is true for the most initial value or case, e.g., for 0 or 1 or another value.

(2)   Assuming that the statement is true in general (e.g., for n), show that it is also true for the incremental case (e.g., for $n + 1$).

Although the rules are simple, there are many useful statements that can be proven by induction.

As an example, consider the formula

$$\sum_{i=1}^{m} i = \frac{m(m+1)}{2},$$

which can be proven by induction as follows. First, consider the initial case $m = 1$. For this value of m, we have

$$\sum_{i=1}^{1} i = \frac{1 \times 2}{2} = 1,$$

and the statement is true. Next, assume that the statement is true for $m = n$, i.e.,

$$\sum_{i=1}^{n} i = \frac{n(n+1)}{2}$$

is given. Then, considering the incremental case $m = (n + 1)$, we have

$$\sum_{i=1}^{n+1} i = \sum_{i=1}^{n} i + (n+1) = \frac{n(n+1)}{2} + (n+1) = \frac{n^2 + 3n + 2}{2} = \frac{(n+1)(n+2)}{2}.$$

Hence,

$$\sum_{i=1}^{n+1} i = \frac{(n+1)(n+2)}{2},$$

and the statement is true for $m = (n+1)$ (if it is true for $m = n$). This completes the proof.

Now, consider the recurrence relation

$$f(m) = f(m-1) + a$$

with initial condition $f(1) = a$. First, we can find the direct formula heuristically. Starting with $f(2) = f(1) + a = a + a = 2a$, we have $f(3) = f(2) + a = 2a + a = 3a$, $f(4) = f(3) + a = 3a + a = 4a$, etc. Hence, $f(m) = ma$ seems to be the direct formula for this sequence, but we need induction to prove it. The initial case $f(1) = a$ is already given, and the formula is satisfied for $m = 1$. We also note that $f(n+1) = f(n) + a$ using the recursive formula. Consequently, if $f(n) = na$, then $f(n+1) = na + a = (n+1)a$, which fits into the direct formula, proving its validity.

As another example, consider the recurrence relation

$$f(m) = a \times f(m-1)$$

with $f(0) = 1$. Note that $f(1) = a \times f(0) = a$, $f(2) = a \times f(1) = a^2$, $f(3) = a \times f(2) = a^3$, etc. Hence, $f(m) = a^m$ seems to be the direct formula, which can be proven again by induction. First, we note that the rule is valid for the initial case $m = 0$, i.e., $f(0) = a^0 = 1$ is already given. Then, using the recursive formula and assuming that $f(n) = a^n$ is correct, we have $f(n+1) = a \times f(n) = a \times a^n = a^{n+1}$, showing that the direct formula is valid.

Finally, consider the recurrence relation

$$f(m) = m \times f(m-1)$$

with $f(0) = 1$. Note that $f(1) = 1 \times f(0) = 1$, $f(2) = 2 \times f(1) = 2$, and $f(3) = 3 \times f(2) = 6$. Hence, $f(m) = m!$ seems to be the direct formula. To prove this, we first note that the rule is valid for $m = 0$, i.e., $f(0) = 1$ is given and correct. Then, using the recursive relation, we write $f(n+1) = (n+1)f(n)$. If $f(n) = n!$, then $f(n+1) = (n+1)n! = (n+1)!$, so that the direct formula is proven to be correct.

As demonstrated in the examples above, the equivalence of a recursive formula and a direct formula can be shown rigorously via proof by induction. The cost of a recursive algorithm often has a recurrence relation, which needs to be converted into a direct expression to assess the algorithm.

3.4 Conclusions

Recursions can be very useful in computer programming. For many problems, the most natural and/or efficient solutions are provided by recursive programs and algorithms. Some examples presented in this chapter are finding the highest common factor and lowest common multiple of a set of integers, Towers of Hanoi, binary search, sequence generation, and computing determinants of matrices. As presented in the next chapters, binomial coefficients can be calculated recursively, and one of the most efficient sorting algorithms, namely the quick sort algorithm, is also based on a recursive structure.

Despite their favorable properties, one should be very careful when implementing recursive algorithms since they can easily go out of control. All recursive structures require termination conditions that must be placed accordingly into programs. Constructing tree structures using simple examples can be very useful when understanding and writing recursive programs. Such a tree structure may also provide some information on the efficiency of a recursive program by showing the depth of recursion in terms of inputs.

3.5 Exercises

1. Write a recursive program that calculates the ith Fibonacci number. Test your code for $i = 10$, $i = 20$, $i = 30$, and $i = 40$. Describe roughly how the processing time changes when i gets larger?

2. Write a recursive program that calculates the factorial of a given number i. Check your code for $i = 10$, $i = 20$, $i = 30$, and $i = 40$ against the built-in function factorial in R. What is the largest i that your program returns a number?

3. Write a recursive program to compute the sum of squares of first n integers. For this purpose, you may use

$$\sum_{i=1}^{n} i^2 = \sum_{i=1}^{n-1} i^2 + n^2$$

for $n > 1$. Hence, the recursive formula to be programmed is $f(n) = f(n-1) + n^2$, where $f(1) = 1$. Test your code for some values of n. Note that the direct formula (that can be used as a reference) is

$$\sum_{i=1}^{n} i^2 = \frac{n(n+1)(2n+1)}{6}.$$

4. Write a recursive program that finds the highest common factor of two nonnegative integers i and j using the Euclidean algorithm. Test your code for the following pairs of (i, j): $(3, 2)$, $(4, 2)$, $(40, 24)$, $(120, 45)$, and $(540, 56)$.

5. Write a recursive program that finds the lowest common multiple of two positive integers i and j, employing the program of the previous question. Test your code for the following pairs of (i, j): $(12, 27)$, $(16, 28)$, $(14, 15)$, $(7, 13)$, $(8, 48)$.

6. Write a recursive program that finds the lowest common multiple of a vector of positive integers, employing the program of the previous question. Test your program for a vector

$$\begin{bmatrix} 700 \\ 50 \\ 4 \\ 3 \\ 2 \end{bmatrix}.$$

7. Write a recursive program to compute the number of movements to solve Towers of Hanoi involving n disks using $f(n) = 2f(n-1) + 1$, where $f(1) = 1$. Test your code for some values of n. Note that the direct formula (that can be used as a reference) is $f(n) = 2^n - 1$.

8. What is the determinant of an $n \times n$ diagonal matrix A ($A[i, j] = 0$ if $i \neq j$)? How the recursive program given in this chapter works for diagonal matrices? How would you change it for a more efficient calculation of the determinant of a diagonal matrix?

Complexity of Programs and Algorithms

4

As briefly discussed in the previous chapters, there are usually several algorithms to solve a given problem. For example, the 1-norm of a vector can be calculated using a loop (`for` or `while`, depending on programming) or a recursion. Hence, for any problem, it is essential to compare different algorithms in terms of efficiency (processing time and memory requirement) and/or accuracy.

In order to compare the efficiency of programs and algorithms, we need to analyze them by estimating or measuring their time and/or memory costs. Estimations are as important as measurements because we often need to know the cost of a program before writing and using it. In addition, we would like to know the cost when different computers are used, rather than relying on a measurement on a specific computer. Consequently, it is not surprising that calculating the costs of programs and algorithms has become a major area in computer science.

Today, performances of computers are usually expressed by an important quantity, namely, floating-point operations per second (FLOPS). This is simply the number of floating-point operations that can be performed in one second. A floating-point operation can be defined as a basic operation, e.g., addition, subtraction, multiplication, or division, applied to floating-point representations of numbers in computers. Hence, to estimate the time cost of a computer program (and hence the underlying algorithm), it would be convenient to count the number of floating-point operations in it. On the other hand, this would be an incomplete estimation since other kinds of operations, such as conditional statements, loop statements, and equalities are ignored. Estimation of the memory cost is usually easier, since one can count the number of scalars and elements in vectors and matrices. But, the memory requirement depends on how the numbers are represented, e.g., single precision or double precision.

In this chapter, we use a systematic approach to understand and estimate costs of programs and algorithms. First, we start with a rigorous analysis by counting each operation and each piece of storage in programs. When these costs are stated as functions of input sizes (and sometimes input values), the resulting expressions are called time and memory *complexities*. Then, we simplify these expressions using asymptotic techniques, leading to a very important concept, namely, the *order*. After

Ö. Ergül, *Guide to Programming and Algorithms Using R*,
DOI 10.1007/978-1-4471-5328-3_4,
© Springer-Verlag London 2013

some practice, we derive shortcuts to explore the costs of programs. Finally, we study the costs of recursive programs, followed by some discussions on orders of various programs and algorithms.

4.1   Complexity of Programs

In our rigorous analysis for the time complexity, we count all lines and operations one by one, except the following cases:

- First lines (function definitions) and output lines (e.g., `return`) are not counted.
- Lines including only { and } are not counted.
- Conditional statements `else` and `else if` are assumed to be connected to the associated `if` statements, and hence they are not counted.

These rules are defined for simplification purposes, and they are not critical, as will be revealed later.

For the memory complexity, we consider all items (inputs, outputs, constants, variables) and count all elements (scalars and all elements in vectors and matrices).

4.1.1   Example: Inner Product

Consider the calculation of the inner product of two given vectors v and $w \in \mathbb{R}^n$. Their inner product is defined as

$$v \cdot w = \sum_{i=1}^{n} v[i]w[i].$$

The following program can be used for this purpose:

```
R Program: Calculation of Inner Product (Original)

01 innerproduct = function(v,w){
02     sumvalue = 0
03     for (i in 1:length(v)){
04         sumvalue = sumvalue + v[i]*w[i]
05     }
06     return(sumvalue)
07 }
```

Now, let us calculate the time cost of this program in terms of n (input size). Except the first and last three lines, we need to work on each line separately. First, consider line 02,

```
sumvalue = 0
```

This is simply setting the variable sumvalue to zero. We do not know how many seconds this operation requires, and in fact, it depends on the computer that we are employing this program. Hence, the only thing we can do is writing the required time for the execution of this line as T_{02}.

Line 03 is a for statement

```
for (i in 1:length(v)){
```

that can be interpreted as the variable i is incremented one by one and compared to the maximum allowed value length(v). Hence, this line is executed for $n + 1$ times with one additional step required for a final comparison to terminate the loop. Then, the overall time required is $(n + 1)T_{03}$, where T_{03} is the time for a single execution of the line, depending again on the computer.

Finally, line 04,

```
sumvalue = sumvalue + v[i]*w[i]
```

is executed for n times since it is inside the loop, and the overall time required for this line is nT_{04}.

Combining all contributions from line 02 to line 04, we obtain the time complexity of the program as

$$T_{all} = T_{02} + (n + 1)T_{03} + nT_{04} = n(T_{03} + T_{04}) + T_{02} + T_{03}.$$

The final equality is particularly important, since one can deduce that $T_{all} \approx n(T_{03} + T_{04})$ when n is large.

Next, let us calculate the memory cost of the program. The program requires the storage of the scalars i and sumvalue, as well as the vectors v and w of size n. Then, the memory complexity should be

$$M_{all} = nM_r + nM_r + M_r + M_r = (2n + 2)M_r,$$

where M_r is the memory required for a real number. Note that $M_{all} \approx 2nM_r$ for large values of n.

At this stage, assume that we would like to write a slightly better program to calculate the inner product of two vectors. Since the inner product is not defined when the vectors have different numbers of elements, we modify the previous program as follows:

```
R Program: Calculation of Inner Product With Check (Original)

01 innerproductwithcheck = function(v,w){
02     if (length(v) == length(w)){
03         sumvalue = 0
04         for (i in 1:length(v)){
05             sumvalue = sumvalue + v[i]*w[i]
06         }
07         return(sumvalue)
08     }
09     else{
10         print("Vectors must have the same length!")
11     }
12 }
```

Now, it is not trivial to find the time complexity of this program since it depends on the inputs v and w. Specifically, if these vectors have different lengths, the program cannot calculate the inner product, and it only prints the warning message in line 10. In this case, the program is quite fast and efficient, although there is not any useful output. On the other hand, when v and w have the same length, the program calculates the inner product that should require significantly longer time and slightly more memory. This situation is called the *worst case*, i.e., the scenario when the inputs are difficult so that the program requires the longest possible time and/or the largest amount of memory. For the program above, the worst case occurs when the vectors have the same length and the inner product is to be calculated.

When finding the complexity of a program, it is possible to construct the analysis on a best-case scenario, a worst-case scenario, or an average-case scenario. But, in order to obtain strict upper bounds for the processing time and memory, it is usually essential to carry out a worst-case analysis. Considering the worst-case scenario for the program above, the time complexity is

$$T_{all} = T_{02} + T_{03} + (n+1)T_{04} + nT_{05} = n(T_{04} + T_{05}) + T_{02} + T_{03} + T_{04},$$

which is almost the same as the time complexity of the previous program. The only difference is the additional time required for the new conditional statement in line 02. Since no new variable is added to the program, the memory complexity is exactly the same as before, i.e., it is

$$M_{all} = (2n+2)M_r.$$

4.2   Order of Complexities

When investigating programs and algorithm, long expressions for time and memory complexities are often replaced with their orders. There are three important reasons:

- Expressions for time and memory complexities include input sizes. Hence, they are useful to estimate the required processing time and memory for given inputs. On the other hand, there are still unknown quantities, such as the actual time in seconds to execute a line or the actual memory in bytes to store a real number. These can be, of course, measured on any computer. However, those values obtained on a computer depend on its capabilities, e.g., its processors. Hence, they may not be very useful if a program is employed on another computer, which has not been used before. Including computer specifications as parameters also complicates the comparisons of programs.
- When comparing programs and assessing their efficiency, it is usually required to know their performances for large input sizes. This is because the efficiency of a program is not critical for small inputs, i.e., when the processing time and required memory are already negligible. Instead, we would like to know what happens when the input size gets larger and the program needs to deal with large data structures.

- Since an algorithm can be programmed in different ways, computing the exact cost of a program includes unnecessary details such as the time required to execute one or more extra lines, conditional statements, etc. Rather than these relatively unimportant information on the programming style or similar small variations, we are more interested in the efficiency of underlying algorithms.

These items above motivate an asymptotic analysis to find the order of a given complexity.

In the literature, the complexity of a program may refer to a detailed expression or its asymptotic order. But, the complexity of an algorithm usually refers to its order.

4.2.1 Order Notation

Let us first construct the mathematical basis for the asymptotic analysis. Let $f(n)$ and $g(n)$ be two functions for $n \in \mathbb{R}$. Then,

$$f(n) = \mathcal{O}(g(n)) \quad \text{as } n \to \infty$$

if and only if there exist positive real numbers C_l and C_h and a real number n_0 such that

$$C_l|g(n)| \leq |f(n)| \leq C_h|g(n)| \quad \text{for all } n > n_0.$$

This expression, i.e., $f(n) = \mathcal{O}(g(n))$, is known as the big-theta notation and can be read as "$f(n)$ is in the order of $g(n)$." The aim is to represent the behavior of $f(n)$ when n gets larger.

Using the definition above immediately leads to two combination methods. Let $f_1(n) = \mathcal{O}(g_1(n))$ and $f_2(n) = \mathcal{O}(g_2(n))$ be positive functions. It can be shown that
- $f_1(n)f_2(n) = \mathcal{O}(g_1(n)g_2(n))$, and
- $f_1(n) + f_2(n) = \mathcal{O}(g_1(n) + g_2(n))$.

Hence, in practice, order expressions can be combined easily. These equalities, as well as the original definition itself, can be used to simplify complex expressions and to find their orders. Also note that, in programming, n is defined as an integer, and time and memory complexities of programs and algorithms are positive functions by default.

As an example, consider a polynomial function

$$f(n) = a_k n^k + a_{k-1} n^{k-1} + a_{k-2} n^{k-2} + \cdots + a_1 n + a_0,$$

where the coefficients a_l for $0 \leq l \leq k$ are all positive. For $n \geq 1$,

$$n^k \geq n^{k-1} \geq n^{k-2} \geq \cdots \geq n \geq 1,$$

leading to

$$a_k n^k \leq f(n) \leq a_k n^k + a_{k-1} n^k + a_{k-2} n^k + \cdots + a_1 n^k + a_0 n^k$$

Fig. 4.1 Some functions in a log–log plot

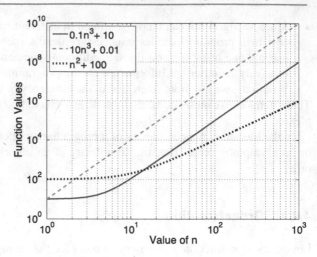

or

$$a_k n^k \le f(n) \le n^k (a_k + a_{k-1} + a_{k-2} + \cdots + a_1 + a_0).$$

Then, letting $C_l = a_k$ and $C_h = (a_k + a_{k-1} + a_{k-2} + \cdots + a_1 + a_0)$, we have

$$C_l n^k \le f(n) \le C_h n^k.$$

The last inequality fits into the definition of the order, and we have $f(n) = \mathcal{O}(n^k)$.

Now, consider the following functions and their orders:

- $f_1(n) = 0.1n^3 + 10 = \mathcal{O}(n^3)$
- $f_2(n) = 10n^3 + 0.01 = \mathcal{O}(n^3)$
- $f_3(n) = n^2 + 100 = \mathcal{O}(n^2)$

These functions are depicted in Fig. 4.1 in a log–log plot, i.e., when x and y axis values of the plot increase logarithmically. These types of plots are useful since functions with different orders can be compared easily. Specifically, in a log–log plot, scaling a function corresponds a shift in the y direction, whereas the slope of a curve represents its power. In this example, both f_1 and f_2 have the same order, i.e., $\mathcal{O}(n^3)$. This means that both functions behave like n^3 since this term dominates as n goes to infinity. In Fig. 4.1, this behavior is visible since both functions have the same slope. Note that the order does not indicate anything about *the constant in front* of the dominant term. These constants (0.1 for f_1 and 10 for f_2) are visible as a difference in the y direction for large values of n. As opposed to others, the order of f_3 is n^2, leading to a lower slope for this function. In other words, since its order is smaller, this function has lower values compared to f_1 and f_2 for sufficiently large values of n. As also shown in Fig. 4.1, different functions may have different behaviors for small values of n, but while analyzing algorithms, we are interested in behaviors and comparisons when n is large.

Following the discussion above, different functions (e.g., complexities) can be compared in the context of order as follows:

- If a function $f_1(n)$ has a higher order than $f_2(n)$, $f_1(n)$ is larger than $f_2(n)$ for sufficiently large values of n. When comparing two programs or algorithms, the one with a lower order can be said to be more efficient than the other.
- If two functions $f_1(n)$ and $f_2(n)$ have the same order, the constants of the dominant terms are required to compare the functions for large values of n. Note that this is not possible if only the order is available. Programs and algorithms having the same order are often said to have the same efficiency, even though the constants, if available, may provide more precise (but less critical) information.

When finding orders of programs and algorithms from their complexities, we usually use shortcuts without using the formal definition detailed above. The strategy is finding the most significant term (e.g., with the highest power of n) and omitting its constant. When doing this, we should keep in mind that this is not an approximation and there is in fact an underlying procedure as described above.

Before working on shortcuts, we emphasize that the formal definition is always available if we are not sure about the most significant term in a given expression. Consider the following two functions:

- $f_1(n) = 2n + 3\log_2(n) = \mathcal{O}(n)$
- $f_2(n) = 3n + 4n\log_2(n) = \mathcal{O}(n\log_2 n)$

For the first example, $\log_2(n) < n$ for $n > 1$, and hence $2n \le f_1(n) \le 5n$ for $n > 1$. Therefore, $f_1(n) = \mathcal{O}(n)$. For the second example, $\log_2(n) > 1$ for $n > 2$, and hence $4n\log_2(n) \le f_2(n) \le 7n\log_2(n)$ for $n > 2$. Therefore, $f_2(n) = \mathcal{O}(n\log_2 n)$.

When discussing orders, the base of a logarithm is often omitted. This is because all logarithms are the same in the context of order. In other words,

$$\mathcal{O}(\log_2 n) = \mathcal{O}(\log_3 n) = \mathcal{O}(\log_4 n) = \cdots .$$

Hence, for the second function above, one can write $f_2(n) = \mathcal{O}(n\log n)$.

4.2.2 Example: Revisiting Inner Product

Consider the following program to calculate again the inner product of two vectors of size n:

```
R Program: Calculation of Inner Product (Revisited)

01 innerproduct = function(v,w){
02     sumvalue = 0
03     n = length(v)
04     for (i in 1:n){
05         sumvalue = sumvalue + v[i]*w[i]
06     }
07     return(sumvalue)
08 }
```

It can be shown that the time complexity of this program is

$$T_{\text{all}} = n(T_{04} + T_{05}) + T_{02} + T_{03} + T_{04},$$

which depends on the value of n. Considering the most significant term, i.e., $n(T_{04} + T_{05})$, we conclude that

$$T_{all} = \mathcal{O}(n).$$

Similarly,

$$M_{all} = (2n + 3)M_r = \mathcal{O}(n).$$

Hence, the time and memory complexities of this program and algorithm (computing the inner product by multiplying elements and adding them) are of order n.

4.2.3 Example: Revisiting Infinity Norm

Now, lets consider the calculation of the ∞-norm of a given vector $v \in \mathbb{R}^n$:

```
R Program: Calculation of Infinity-Norm (Revisited)

01 infinitynorm = function(v){
02    maxvalue = 0
03    n = length(v)
04    for (i in 1:n){
05        if (abs(v[i]) > maxvalue){
06            maxvalue = abs(v[i])
07        }
08    }
09    return(maxvalue)
10 }
```

It can be shown that, in the worst case, the time complexity of this program is

$$T_{all} = n(T_{04} + T_{05} + T_{06}) + T_{02} + T_{03} + T_{04}.$$

Note that the values of T_{02}, T_{03}, T_{04}, T_{05}, and T_{06} are not the same as those used before. Considering the variables `maxvalue`, `n`, `i`, as well as the input vector `v`, the memory complexity is

$$M_{all} = (n + 3)M_r.$$

Considering the significant terms involving n, the time and memory complexities of this program are also $\mathcal{O}(n)$.

According to our analysis, the complexity (both time and memory) of calculating the inner product is $\mathcal{O}(n)$. This means that when n gets larger, the cost of the program increases linearly. For example, increasing the value of n by a factor of two (approximately) increases the processing time and memory by factors of two. The complexity of the infinite norm is also $\mathcal{O}(n)$, but this does not mean that the two programs (and the corresponding algorithms) have precisely the same cost. This only indicates that the cost of the infinite norm is also linear, i.e., increasing the value of n by a factor of two (approximately) increases the processing time and memory by factors of two.

4.2.4 Example: Revisiting Matrix–Vector Multiplication

Consider the multiplication of a matrix $A \in \mathbb{R}^{m \times n}$ with a vector $x \in \mathbb{R}^n$ using the program below.

```
R Program: Matrix-Vector Multiplication (Revisited)

01 matvecmult = function(A,x){
02     m = nrow(A)
03     n = ncol(A)
04     y = matrix(0,nrow=m)
05     for (i in 1:m){
06         sumvalue = 0
07         for (j in 1:n){
08             sumvalue = sumvalue + A[i,j]*x[j]
09         }
10         y[i] = sumvalue
11     }
12     return(y)
13 }
```

Lets first find the time cost of this program. Lines 02 to 04 are executed only once. Hence, we can start by adding the time required for these lines as

$$T_{all} = T_{02} + T_{03} + T_{04} + \cdots.$$

Line 05 is a for statement, which is executed for $m + 1$ times, including a final check of the variable i, leading to

$$T_{all} = T_{02} + T_{03} + T_{04} + (m + 1)T_{05} + \cdots.$$

In addition, lines 06 and 10 are inside this loop and executed for m times, which can be added as

$$T_{all} = T_{02} + T_{03} + T_{04} + (m + 1)T_{05} + mT_{06} + mT_{10} + \cdots.$$

At this stage, we need to focus on the inner loop. Line 07 is a for statement, which is executed for $n + 1$ times for each i. Hence, this line is executed for a total of $m(n + 1)$ times, leading to

$$T_{all} = T_{02} + T_{03} + T_{04} + (m + 1)T_{05} + mT_{06} + mT_{10} + m(n + 1)T_{07} + \cdots.$$

Finally, the contribution of line 08 can be added as

$$T_{all} = T_{02} + T_{03} + T_{04} + (m + 1)T_{05} + mT_{06} + mT_{10} + m(n + 1)T_{07} + mnT_{08}.$$

Rearranging the terms, we obtain a final expression for the time complexity as

$$T_{all} = mn(T_{07} + T_{08}) + m(T_{05} + T_{06} + T_{07} + T_{10}) + T_{02} + T_{03} + T_{04} + T_{05}.$$

Table 4.1 Items used in the matrix–vector multiplication program

Item	Type	Number of elements
A	Input	mn
x	Input	n
y	Output	m
m	Variable	1
n	Variable	1
sumvalue	Variable	1

As opposed to the previous examples, the time complexity of the matrix–vector multiplication involves two variables, i.e., the number of rows m and the number of columns n. In order to find the order of this complexity, we again take the most significant term so that

$$T_{all} = \mathcal{O}(mn).$$

For the memory complexity of the matrix–vector multiplication, let us make a simple table (Table 4.1) showing all items used in the program.

Adding all contributions, we have

$$M_{all} = mn + n + m + 3 = \mathcal{O}(mn).$$

Both time and memory complexities of the matrix–vector multiplication are $\mathcal{O}(mn)$. Different cases can be considered now:

- When $m \approx n$, i.e., when the numbers of columns and rows are nearly the same, $\mathcal{O}(mn) = \mathcal{O}(n^2)$, which can be interpreted as the complexity of the matrix–vector multiplication has a quadratic order.
- When m is constant, $\mathcal{O}(mn) = \mathcal{O}(n)$. In this case, the cost of the matrix–vector multiplication is investigated as the number of columns is increased, i.e., the matrix becomes wider and wider. Note that, having a very large m does not change the order, as long as it is defined as a constant.
- When n is constant, $\mathcal{O}(mn) = \mathcal{O}(m)$. In this case, the cost of the matrix–vector multiplication is investigated as the number of rows are increased, i.e., the matrix becomes longer and longer. Again note that a very large n does not change the order as long as it is defined as a constant.
- When $m = 1$ or $n = 1$, the matrix–vector multiplication reduces into an inner product of two vectors. In these cases, the complexity is $\mathcal{O}(n)$ or $\mathcal{O}(m)$, depending on which one is considered as a constant.

As a demonstration, Table 4.2 lists the results of an experiment using the matrix–vector multiplication program for square matrices with different sizes. Since we performing time measurements and inputs/outputs are not critical (provided that the program works smoothly), we select all elements of the matrices and input vectors as unity. The measurements are performed for $n = 100$, $n = 200$, $n = 400$, $n = 800$, and $n = 1600$. Table 4.2 shows the processing time in seconds, which can be measured using the built-in `system.time` function of R. We also list the increase rate, i.e., the ratio between the processing times in consecutive runs, for $n \geq 100$.

Table 4.2 Measurements for matrix–vector multiplications with square matrices

n	Processing time (seconds)	Increase rate
100	0.038	–
200	0.127	3.34
400	0.651	5.13
800	2.650	4.07
1600	10.482	3.96

It can be observed that the increase rate approaches 4 as n gets larger. Hence, this experiment confirms our analysis, which states that the order of the matrix–vector multiplication is $\mathcal{O}(n^2)$. Specifically, for large values of n, we expect that doubling the value of n should increase the processing time by $2^2 = 4$ times. This is clearly visible in Table 4.2.

In the experiment above, the increase rate is quite different from 4 when n is small. There are two reasons for this:

- As analyzed before, the time complexity of the program is

$$T_{all} = mn(T_{07} + T_{08}) + m(T_{05} + T_{06} + T_{07} + T_{10}) + T_{02} + T_{03} + T_{04} + T_{05},$$

    which becomes

$$T_{all} = n^2(T_{07} + T_{08}) + n(T_{05} + T_{06} + T_{07} + T_{10}) + T_{02} + T_{03} + T_{04} + T_{05}$$

    for $m = n$. Obviously, in addition to the most significant term with n^2, there are other terms (e.g., with n), whose contributions are visible for small values of n.
- When the execution of a program is faster, the time measurement is less reliable since a shorter processing time is to be measured. All time measurements are contaminated by some factors, such as out-of-control system programs running on the same computer, but this contamination becomes more visible in shorter durations.

Nevertheless, we need to emphasize again that measurements are not critical for small values of n, i.e., when processing times are short and tolerable, and when their accurate prediction is not needed.

4.3 Shortcuts for Finding Orders of Programs

When the order of a complexity is found from its full expression, the most dominant term is extracted, and its constant is omitted to obtain a simplified expression. Then, the following question arises: Can we find a way to derive the order directly from the program without finding and simplifying the full expression for the complexity? The answer is positive, provided that we investigate the given program carefully to find out critical lines (for processing time) and critical items (for memory).

As an example, consider the following program for the multiplication of a matrix $A \in \mathbb{R}^{m \times n}$ with a vector $x \in \mathbb{R}^n$.

```
R Program: Matrix–Vector Multiplication (Revisited)

01 matvecmult = function(A,x){
02    m = nrow(A)
03    n = ncol(A)
04    y = matrix(0,nrow=m)
05    for (i in 1:m){
06       sumvalue = 0
07       for (j in 1:n){
08          sumvalue = sumvalue + A[i,j]*x[j]
09       }
10       y[i] = sumvalue
11    }
12    return(y)
13 }
```

To find the order of the time complexity, we find a line that is inside all loops and executed more than others. For the program above, line 08, i.e.,

```
sumvalue = sumvalue + A[i,j]*x[j]
```

fits into this definition. Then, we find how many times this critical line is executed. Since line 08 is inside an outer loop (i from 1 to m) and an inner loop (j from 1 to n), it is executed for a total of mn times. Omitting all constants and smaller terms that may arise at this stage, the number of times that the line is executed corresponds to the order of the time complexity. There is no such extra term in mn, and hence one can immediately conclude that the time complexity of the matrix–vector multiplication is $\mathcal{O}(mn)$.

Note that, in the program above, one can also select line 07 as a critical line. This line is executed for $m(n + 1) = mn + m$ times. But, omitting m compared to mn, we again reach the same expression, i.e., $\mathcal{O}(mn)$, for the time complexity.

To find the order of the memory complexity, we find the item (input, output, variable, or constant) that has the largest number of elements. For the program above, this item is the matrix A, which has a total of mn elements. Therefore, the memory complexity of the matrix–vector multiplication is also $\mathcal{O}(mn)$.

4.3.1 Example: Matrix–Matrix Multiplication

Consider now the multiplication of two matrices $A \in \mathbb{R}^{m \times n}$ and $B \in \mathbb{R}^{n \times p}$:

```
R Program: Matrix–Matrix Multiplication (Original)

01 matmatmult = function(A,B) {
02     m = nrow(A)
03     n = ncol(A)
04     p = ncol(B)
05     C = matrix(0,nrow=m,ncol=p)
06     for (i in 1:m) {
07         for (j in 1:p) {
08             sumvalue = 0
09             for (k in 1:n) {
10                 sumvalue = sumvalue + A[i,k]*B[k,j]
11             }
12             C[i,j] = sumvalue
13         }
14     }
15     return(C)
16 }
```

To find the order of the time complexity, we note that line 10 is a critical line. This line is executed for mpn times, and hence the time complexity is $\mathcal{O}(mpn)$. For the memory complexity, we need to consider three major matrices, i.e., A, B, and C. These matrices involve mn, np, and mp elements, respectively. Considering that m, n, and p can be arbitrary, we conclude that the memory complexity is $\mathcal{O}(mn + np + mp)$ in general. Using these expressions for square matrices, i.e., for $m = p = n$, the time and memory complexities of the matrix–matrix multiplication are $\mathcal{O}(n^3)$ and $\mathcal{O}(n^2)$, respectively. Note that, for the memory complexity in this case, we have

$$\mathcal{O}(n^2 + n^2 + n^2) = \mathcal{O}(3n^2) = \mathcal{O}(n^2).$$

When $p = 1$, both the time and memory complexities of the matrix–matrix multiplication are $\mathcal{O}(mn)$, which is consistent with our previous analysis for the complexity of the matrix–vector multiplication. Another special case occurs when $m = 1$ and $n = 1$, corresponding to the inner product of two vectors of size p, with $\mathcal{O}(p)$ time and memory complexities.

4.4   Complexity and Order of Recursive Programs and Algorithms

Up to now, we have seen how to estimate costs of various programs and algorithms. We also discussed some shortcuts to derive orders by finding critical lines and their repetitions. On the other hand, problems arise when considering recursive programs and algorithms. Unsurprisingly, the cost of a recursive program or algorithm also has a recursive expression, which needs to be solved to get an explicit (direct) expression.

As an example, lets consider the recursive calculation of the 1-norm of a given vector $v \in \mathbb{R}^n$ using the following program:

R Program: Recursive Calculation of 1-Norm (Revisited)

```
01 onenormrecursive = function(v){
02     if (length(v) > 1){
03         sum1 = onenormrecursive(v[1:floor(length(v)/2)])
04         sum2 = onenormrecursive(v[(floor(length(v)/2)+1):length(v)])
05         sumvalue = sum1 + sum2
06     }
07     else{
08         sumvalue = abs(v[1])
09     }
10     return(sumvalue)
11 }
```

In order to simplify the analysis of the time complexity, assume that $n = 2^a$ for an integer a (hence $a = \log_2 n$). Considering that line 02 (connected to line 07) and line 05 are executed, in addition to two calls of the program itself (with smaller vectors of $n/2 = 2^{a-1}$ elements), we have

$$T_{\text{all}}(2^a) = T_{02} + T_{05} + 2T_{\text{all}}(2^{a-1}) \quad \text{or} \quad T_{\text{all}}(n) = T_{02} + T_{05} + 2T_{\text{all}}(n/2)$$

for the time complexity. Then, we obtain a recurrence relation as $T_{\text{all}}(n) = C + 2T_{\text{all}}(n/2)$, where $C = T_{02} + T_{05}$ is a constant (does not depend on n). Note that the processing times required for lines 03 and 04 are both $T_{\text{all}}(n/2)$, which is the time required to execute the function itself for vectors of size $n/2$. Some extra time may be required as the numerical results of function calls are assigned to variables sum1 and sum2. Specifically, the assignments in lines 03 and 04 may have some contributions in the overall time complexity. But, such an extra time is constant (say T_{add}), and the final recurrence relation still holds, i.e., we have

$$T_{\text{all}}(n) = C + 2T_{\text{all}}(n/2)$$

for some constant $C = T_{02} + T_{05} + T_{\text{add}}$. Considering large values of n, one can write a sequence of equations as

$$
\begin{aligned}
T_{\text{all}}(n) &= C + 2T_{\text{all}}(n/2) \\
&= C + 2(C + 2T_{\text{all}}(n/4)) = C + 2C + 4T_{\text{all}}(n/4) \\
&= C + 2C + 4(C + 2T_{\text{all}}(n/8)) = C + 2C + 4C + 8T_{\text{all}}(n/8) \\
&\vdots \\
&= C + 2C + 4C + 8C + \cdots + \frac{n}{2}CT_{\text{all}}(2) \\
&= C + 2C + 4C + 8C + \cdots + \frac{n}{2}C + nT_{\text{all}}(1) \\
&= C + 2C + 4C + 8C + \cdots + \frac{n}{2}C + n(T_{02} + T_{08}) \\
&= C \sum_{i=0}^{a-1} 2^i + nD,
\end{aligned}
$$

where $D = T_{02} + T_{08}$ represents the processing time when the input vector has only one element. Evaluating the final summation, we get the order of the time complexity as

$$T_{all}(n) = \frac{1 - 2^a}{1 - 2}C + nD = nC + nD - C = \mathcal{O}(n).$$

The analysis of the memory complexity of a recursive algorithm is slightly tricky. One needs to separate the memory used for the initial input, because it is allocated just once. For the program above, putting v aside, we have the recurrence relation

$$M_{others}(n) = C + 2M_{others}(n/2),$$

where C accounts for the scalar variables. An analysis similar to the one above leads to $M_{others}(n) = \mathcal{O}(n)$. Combining this with the memory for the input, we have

$$M_{all}(n) = M_{input}(n) + M_{others}(n) = \mathcal{O}(n) + M_{others}(n) = \mathcal{O}(n) + \mathcal{O}(n) = \mathcal{O}(n)$$

as the memory complexity of the program.

Now, consider the following program with some modifications on the original one:

```
R Program: Recursive Calculation of 1-Norm (Inefficient)

01 onenormrecursive = function(v){
02     if (length(v) > 1){
03         w = v[1:floor(length(v)/2)]
04         z = v[(floor(length(v)/2)+1):length(v)]
05         sum1 = onenormrecursive(w)
06         sum2 = onenormrecursive(z)
07         sumvalue = sum1 + sum2
08     }
09     else{
10         sumvalue = abs(v[1])
11     }
12     return(sumvalue)
13 }
```

In this program, the input vector v is explicitly divided into two vectors w and z to be used when the program is called. Unfortunately, this means extra memory in each recursion step. To be specific, we have

$$M_{others}(n) = C + nD + 2M_{others}(n/2),$$

leading to the sequence

$$M_{others}(n) = C + nD + 2M_{others}(n/2)$$
$$= C + nD + 2(C + nD/2 + 2M_{others}(n/4))$$
$$= C + 2C + 2nD + 4M_{others}(n/4)$$

$$\vdots$$

$$= C + 2C + 4C + 8C + \cdots + \frac{n}{2}C + anD + nM_{\text{others}} \quad (1)$$

$$= C \sum_{i=0}^{a-1} 2^i + (n \log_2 n)D + nE$$

$$= nC - C + (n \log_2 n)D + nE$$

$$= \mathcal{O}(n \log_2 n).$$

Combining this result with the memory for the initial input vector, we have

$$M_{\text{all}}(n) = \mathcal{O}(n) + M_{\text{others}}(n) = \mathcal{O}(n) + \mathcal{O}(n \log_2 n) = \mathcal{O}(n \log_2 n) = \mathcal{O}(n \log n)$$

as the memory complexity of the program. Hence, the program above has a higher memory complexity than the original one, i.e., it is more inefficient, even though both programs are based on the same recursive algorithm. As shown in this example, memory used for some new variables may accumulate in a recursive program, even leading to increase in the order of the memory complexity.

4.4.1   Example: Revisiting Binary Search

Let us consider the recursive binary-search algorithm and revisit the following program, which finds the position of a given number in a vector $v \in \mathbb{R}^n$ involving sorted numbers.

```
R Program: Recursive Binary Search (Revisited)

01 binarysearchrecursive = function(v,thenumber,lowerindex,higherindex){
02     if (lowerindex > higherindex){
03         print("The number is not found!")
04     }
05     else{
06         middleindex = lowerindex + floor((higherindex-lowerindex)/2)
07         if (v[middleindex] == thenumber){
08             return(middleindex)
09         }
10         else if (v[middleindex] < thenumber){
11             binarysearchrecursive(v,thenumber,middleindex+1,higherindex)
12         }
13         else if (v[middleindex] > thenumber){
14             binarysearchrecursive(v,thenumber,lowerindex,middleindex-1)
15         }
16     }
17 }
```

Assume that the input vector v has $n = 2^a$ elements for an integer a. Considering the worst-case scenario, the searched number thenumber is not found in the first step. Hence, the same algorithm is called again for a vector of size $n/2 = 2^{a-1}$. Before this second call, however, line 02 (connected to line 05), line 06, and line

07 (connected to lines 10 and 13) are executed. Then, we can write the overall time complexity as

$$T_{\text{all}}(2^a) = T_{02} + T_{06} + T_{07} + T_{\text{all}}(2^{a-1}) \quad \text{or} \quad T_{\text{all}}(n) = T_{02} + T_{06} + T_{07} + T_{\text{all}}(n/2).$$

For large values of n, a sequence of equations can be written as

$$T_{\text{all}}(n) = C + T_{\text{all}}(n/2)$$
$$= 2C + T_{\text{all}}(n/4)$$
$$= 3C + T_{\text{all}}(n/8)$$
$$\vdots$$

where C is a constant (does not depend on n).

According to the worst-case scenario, the search does not end until `lowindex` equals `highindex` so that the recursion cannot continue any further. Considering all steps, the time complexity of the program can be written as

$$T_{\text{all}}(n) = aC + T_{\text{all}}(n/2^a) = \log_2(n)C + T_{\text{all}}(1).$$

At this stage, the program stops if the searched number is found. On the other hand, it is possible that the number does not exist in the vector. In this case, line 02 (followed by line 03) is executed once more, but this is not significant in terms of the time cost, and we have $T_{\text{all}}(1) = \mathcal{O}(1)$. Consequently,

$$T_{\text{all}}(n) = \mathcal{O}(\log_2(n)) = \mathcal{O}(\log n),$$

which means that the time complexity of the recursive binary search has a logarithmic order. Note that, despite its logarithmic time complexity, the program above has $\mathcal{O}(n)$ memory complexity since the input v has n elements to be stored.

4.4.2   Example: Revisiting Sequence Generation

Consider the recursive program below, which can be used to list all words with n letters (either "a" and "b").

```
R Program: Generate Words With a and b (Revisited)

01 generateab = function(n){
02    if (n > 0){
03       v = rbind(matrix("a",nrow=2^(n-1)),matrix("b",nrow=2^(n-1)))
04       return(noquote(cbind(v,rbind(generateab(n-1),generateab(n-1)))))
05    }
06 }
```

The output of this program is a matrix of $2^n \times n$ elements. For finding the time complexity, we need to analyze lines 03 and 04 carefully. The time complexity of line 03 depends on the value of n since two vectors of size 2^{n-1} are combined using rbind. We may assume that rbind (and cbind) operations involve combinations of two data structures, where one of them (e.g., smaller one) is moved in memory. Hence, $T_{03} = t_{03}2^{n-1}$, where t_{03} is a constant. In line 04, the program itself is called twice with input n-1. Outputs of these calls are matrices of size $2^{n-1} \times (n-1)$. These matrices are combined using rbind with a time complexity of $T_{04a} = t_{04a}(n-1)2^{n-1}$. Then, the resulting $2^n \times (n-1)$ matrix is combined with a vector of 2^n elements using cbind, which has $T_{04b} = t_{04b}2^n$ time complexity. Considering all contributions, we obtain

$$T_{\text{all}}(n) = t_{03}2^{n-1} + t_{04a}(n-1)2^{n-1} + t_{04b}2^n + 2T_{\text{all}}(n-1)$$

or

$$T_{\text{all}}(n) = (C + nD)2^n + 2T_{\text{all}}(n-1),$$

where

$$C = t_{03}/2 - t_{04a}/2 + t_{04b} \quad \text{and} \quad D = t_{04a}/2.$$

Using the expression above, one can obtain

$$T_{\text{all}}(n) = 2^n \sum_{i=0}^{n-1}(C + (n-i)D) = (C + nD/2 + n^2D/2)2^n$$

or

$$T_{\text{all}}(n) = \mathcal{O}(n^2 2^n) = \mathcal{O}(2^{p(n)}),$$

where $p(n) = n + 2\log_2 n$. Hence, the time complexity of the sequence generation has an exponential order, as discussed in the next setion. Carrying out a similar analysis, it can be shown that the memory complexity of the program above also has an exponential order.

4.5   Orders of Various Algorithms

As we analyzed in this chapter, the inner product of two vectors and the computation of the infinite norm of a vector have $\mathcal{O}(n)$ time and memory complexities, whereas the matrix–vector multiplication has $\mathcal{O}(n^2)$ complexity for square matrices. Similarly, for $n \times n$ square matrices, the matrix–matrix multiplication has $\mathcal{O}(n^3)$ time complexity and $\mathcal{O}(n^2)$ memory complexity. Therefore, all these programs and algorithms have polynomial orders, since n, n^2, and n^3 are polynomials.

In general, a program or algorithm has a *polynomial order* if its complexity is $\mathcal{O}(n^k)$ for some constant $k > 0$, where n is the input size. As special cases, $k = 1$, $k = 2$, and $k = 3$ correspond to the linear, quadratic, and cubic orders, respectively. Note that the case $k = 0$ is not considered as a polynomial order since $\mathcal{O}(n^0) = \mathcal{O}(1)$ indicates another family of programs and algorithms with constant orders.

Fig. 4.2 Processing time as a function of input size for four hypothetical algorithms

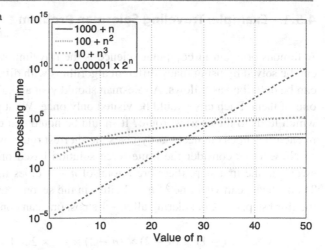

In addition to those with polynomial orders, there are many programs and algorithms with logarithmic and exponential orders. A program or algorithm has a *logarithmic order* if its complexity is $\mathcal{O}(\log n)$ and has an *exponential order* if its complexity is $\mathcal{O}(2^{p(n)})$, where $p(n)$ is a polynomial or any function of polynomial order. Similar to the base of the logarithm, the base of the exponential term is not important, but it is often selected as 2. Examples are the recursive binary search with a logarithmic time complexity and recursive sequence generation with exponential time and memory complexities.

In general, programs and algorithms with exponential complexities are considered as expensive, and, if possible, they are avoided (replaced with inexpensive programs and algorithms). Despite this usual warning, there is no a common criterion to directly judge the complexity, and in fact, the assessment of the efficiency often depends on the application area. For example, the Gaussian elimination with $\mathcal{O}(n^3)$ time complexity is a major tool in linear algebra, but it is often considered to be expensive. Therefore, it is replaced with iterative methods and fast algorithms for large n values that are encountered in many practical problems.

As a demonstration, Fig. 4.2 depicts the processing time for four hypothetical programs with different orders. The time complexities of the programs are given as $1000+n$, $100+n^2$, $10+n^3$, and 0.00001×2^n. Note that the y axis has a logarithmic scale, but the x axis has not. We observe that, for small values of n, the slowest and the fastest programs are the first and the fourth, respectively. However, as the value of n increases, the cost of the fourth program increases rapidly (exponentially), and this program becomes the slowest one among four programs for large values of n. Similar comparisons can be made between other programs. Usually, solutions of small problems are not critical, and performances of programs for small input sizes are not important. On the other hand, as the input size increases and solutions become difficult, we need to find the most efficient programs, and this information can be obtained by analyzing complexities and orders of programs and algorithms.

4.5.1 Example: Traveling Salesman Problem

A famous problem in computer science is the traveling salesman problem, which can be solved by using many different algorithms with different costs. The problem can be described as follows. A salesman should visit a total of n cities starting from one of them. Each city should be visited only once. What is the sequence of cities, which leads to the shortest route? It should be noted that choosing the nearest city in each step does not necessarily gives the shortest route overall.

Now, let us consider the brute-force solution based on testing all possible answers. In the first step, there are a total of $n - 1$ cities that the salesman can go. Then, she/he can visit one of $n - 2$ cities in the second step, one of $n - 3$ cities in the third step, etc. Considering all $n - 1$ steps, one can conclude that there are

$$(n - 1) \times (n - 2) \times (n - 3) \times \cdots \times 2 \times 1 = (n - 1)!$$

different choices for the trip. These possible trips can be directly compared with each other and the one with the shortest route can be found. The complexity of this algorithm is clearly $\mathcal{O}(n!)$, i.e., it has a factorial order, which is even worse than the exponential order.

4.5.2 Fibonacci Numbers

Let us consider the calculation of the ith Fibonacci number. One can use the recurrence relation

$$f(i) = f(i - 1) + f(i - 2), \quad i > 2,$$

with conditions $f(1) = 1$ and $f(2) = 1$ to write the following program:

```
R Program: Recursive Calculation of nth Fibonacci Number (Revisited)

01 fiborecursive = function(i){
02     if (i <= 2){
03         return(1)
04     }
05     else{
06         return(fiborecursive(i-1)+fiborecursive(i-2))
07     }
08 }
```

Even though this program seems quite compact and natural (using the definition of the Fibonacci numbers), it is expensive. The time complexity can be written as

$$T_{\text{all}}(i) = C + 2T_{\text{all}}(i - 1),$$

where C is a constant. Note that, in this example, i is not the input size, and the time complexity depends on the value of the input i rather than its size. To find a direct formula for the time cost, a sequence of equations can be derived as

$$T_{\text{all}}(i) = C + 2T_{\text{all}}(i-1)$$
$$= C + 2(C + 2T_{\text{all}}(i-2)) = C + 2C + 4T_{\text{all}}(i-2)$$
$$= C + 2C + 4(C + 2T_{\text{all}}(i-3)) = C + 2C + 4C + 8T_{\text{all}}(i-3)$$

$$\vdots$$

$$= C + 2C + 4C + 8C + \cdots + 2^{i-2}C + 2^{i-1}T_{\text{all}}(1)$$
$$= C + 2C + 4C + 8C + \cdots + 2^{i-2}C + 2^{i-1}T_{02}$$
$$= C\sum_{j=0}^{i-2} 2^j + 2^{i-1}T_{02}$$
$$= 2^{i-1}C - C + 2^{i-1}T_{02},$$

which leads to

$$T_{\text{all}}(i) = \mathcal{O}(2^i).$$

Hence, the time complexity of recursively calculating the ith Fibonacci number has an exponential order.

In order to understand why the simple program above is so expensive, consider the calculation of the 7th Fibonacci number, i.e., $f(7) = f(6) + f(5)$, which requires $f(6)$ and $f(5)$. On the other hand, $f(6) = f(5) + f(4)$, which means that $f(5)$ is calculated twice to find $f(7)$. Similarly, $f(4)$ is calculated three times, $f(3)$ is calculated four times, etc. These duplications in the calculations grow rapidly, leading to an exponential order.

As mentioned in Chap. 3, the cost of a recursive program is often related to the depth of the recursion. On the other hand, the cost may not be directly proportional to the depth, as the cost per recursion level may also change. For the program above, the depth of the recursion is $\mathcal{O}(i)$. But, the cost is doubled from a level to the next level, which leads to an exponential complexity overall.

Following the discussion above, a more efficient algorithm to calculate the ith Fibonacci number can be proposed. In such an algorithm, the Fibonacci numbers from 1 to i can be calculated using the expression $f(i) = f(i-1) + f(i-2)$ in a loop, rather than a recursion. A program using a for loop can be written as follows:

```
    R Program: Iterative Calculation of the nth Fibonacci Number (Original)

01 fiboiterative = function(i){
02      if (i <= 2){
03          value = 1
04      }
05      else{
06          value1 = 1
07          value2 = 1
08          for (j in 3:i){
09              value = value1 + value2
10              value1 = value2
11              value2 = value
12          }
13      }
14      return(value)
15 }
```

In this program, the variables value1 and value2 store the values of two consecutive Fibonacci numbers. For each value of j from 3 to i, the values of these variables are updated appropriately. Specifically, value2 is copied to value1, whereas value2 is updated as the sum of value1 and value2 from the previous step. This way, when the loop finishes,

$$value = value1 + value2$$

gives the ith Fibonacci number.

In the program above, lines 09–11 can be considered as critical lines, which are executed for $i - 2$ times. Therefore, the time complexity of this program is $\mathcal{O}(i)$, which is much better than the exponential complexity of the recursive program and algorithm. Moreover, the memory complexity is $\mathcal{O}(1)$ since only a couple of scalar variables are used. Finally, this program can be considered as a kind of iterative procedure since each iteration depends on previous iterations. In this context, the program converges to the ith Fibonacci number, whereas no divergence is expected.

Once again, we emphasize that programs and algorithms need to be compared extensively in terms of efficiency and/or accuracy. Even for very simple problems, some programs and algorithms can be much better than others.

4.5.3 Binomial Coefficients

Consider the computation of the binomial coefficient

$$b(i, j) = \binom{i}{j} = \frac{i!}{j!(i - j)!}$$

Obviously, this quantity can easily be calculated by using the factorial as follows:

R Program: Finding Binomial Coefficients Using Factorial (Original)

```
01 binomialusingfactorial = function(i,j){
02     value = factorial(i) / ( factorial(j)*factorial(i-j))
03     return(value)
04 }
```

However, this program is unstable. For example, consider the calculation of

$$\binom{200}{199} = \frac{200!}{199!(200-199)!} = 200.$$

Using a standard computer, the program above cannot do this! This is because both 199! and 200! are very large numbers and they cannot be represented properly in R. Hence, the program cannot provide any useful output, although it should be simply 200. Specifically, this instability can be observed when factorials of the inputs i and j are very large. In order to overcome this problem, a more stable program is required.

First, let us consider the Pascal triangle, which directly provides the binomial coefficients. First seven lines of the triangle are as follows:

$$1$$

$$1 \quad 1$$

$$1 \quad 2 \quad 1$$

$$1 \quad 3 \quad 3 \quad 1$$

$$1 \quad 4 \quad 6 \quad 4 \quad 1$$

$$1 \quad 5 \quad 10 \quad 10 \quad 5 \quad 1$$

$$1 \quad 6 \quad 15 \quad 20 \quad 15 \quad 6 \quad 1$$

Each number in a line is the sum of two numbers in the previous line. This way, the Pascal triangle consists of the binomial coefficients, where the coefficient $b(i, j)$ resides at $(j + 1)$th position of the $(i + 1)$th line. For example, check the value of

$$b(6, 3) = \binom{6}{3} = 20$$

residing at the 4th position in the 7th line.

The Pascal triangle provides the required recursion to obtain the binomial coefficients. Specifically, we have

$$b(i, j) = b(i - 1, j - 1) + b(i - 1, j)$$

with $b(0, 0) = 1$, leading to the following stable program.

```
R Program: Finding Binomial Coefficients Using the Pascal Triangle (Original)

01 binomialpascal = function(i,j){
02     if (j = 0){
03         value = 1
04     }
05     else if (i == j){
06         value = 1
07     else{
10         value = binomialpascal(i-1,j-1) + binomialpascal(i-1,j)
11     }
12     return(value)
13 }
```

Although this program (and the underlying algorithm based on the Pascal triangle) is more stable than the previous program (and the underlying algorithm based on factorials), it is very expensive, particularly for the coefficients at the middle of the Pascal triangle. For example, if $j \approx i/2$, then the time complexity of the program above is $\mathcal{O}(2^i)$. Hence, we need better programs and algorithms for both efficient and stable computations of the binomial coefficients.

In order to derive a new algorithm, one can use the expression of the binomial coefficients and perform cancellations to arrive at

$$b(i, j) = \binom{i}{j} = \frac{i!}{j!(i-j)!} = \frac{i \times (i-1) \times (i-2) \times \cdots \times (i-j+1)}{j \times (j-1) \times (j-2) \times \cdots \times 1}.$$

Factorization of the final equality leads to

$$b(i, j) = \frac{i}{j} b(i-1, j-1).$$

This is a very useful recurrence relation that can be implemented as follows:

```
R Program: Finding Binomial Coefficients Recursively (Original)

01 binomialrecursive = function(i,j){
02     if (j == 0){
03         value = 1
04     }
05     else{
08         value = (i/j)*binomialrecursive(i-1,j-1)
09     }
10     return(value)
11 }
```

Similar to the previous program using the Pascal triangle, this program is quite stable. In addition, as a very important advantage, the program above is extremely efficient with only $\mathcal{O}(j)$ time complexity.

Table 4.3 Programs/algorithms to compute binomial coefficients

Program/Algorithm	Time complexity	Behavior for large i
Using Factorial	$\mathcal{O}(i)$	Unstable
Using the Pascal's Triangle	$\mathcal{O}(2^i)$ if $j \approx i/2$	Stable
Recursive	$\mathcal{O}(j)$	Stable

Although less important, the program using the recurrence relation is even better than the program using the Pascal's triangle in terms of stability. The binomial coefficients are often generalized as

$$b(i, j) = 0 \quad \text{if } i < j.$$

Using the programs above for such a case, only the third (using the recurrence relation) may give zero, while the first (using factorials) returns a not-a-number error, and the second (using Pascal's triangle) suffers from an infinite recursion. Hence, if such a case may occur in an application, the first and second programs need to be improved via conditional statements, whereas the program using the recurrence relation does not require any modification.

Finally, we summarize the programs/algorithms to compute the binomial coefficients in Table 4.3. Among three different methods, only the recursive version provides both efficient and stable computations. For the solution of a given problem, the programmers often need to search for the most efficient and most stable/accurate programs and algorithms. In some cases, as in the computation of the binomial coefficients, it may be possible to find a nice algorithm, whose implementation exhibits both efficiency and stability. In some cases, however, the programmer may need to choose between efficiency and stability/accuracy, depending on the application and user needs.

4.6 Conclusions

For a given problem, it is essential to compare different programs and algorithms in terms of efficiency and/or accuracy. Efficiency refers to the speed of programs and algorithms, as well as to the amount of memory required by them. For both speed and memory usage, the efficiency of a program/algorithm naturally depends on its inputs.

This chapter is devoted to estimating processing time and memory costs of computer programs. For a given program, a rigorous approach can be followed by counting each operation and each piece of storage to find the complexity of the program as well as the underlying algorithm. At the same time, we are more interested in the efficiency of programs when input sizes/values are large so that time and memory costs are significant. This leads to an asymptotic analysis to find orders from complexities and to use the resulting neat expressions for assessing the efficiency of implementations. This chapter also discusses some shortcuts to calculate the orders of programs and algorithms by finding critical lines and items in the codes.

4.7   Exercises

1. Write a program that calculates the inner product of two given vectors v and $w \in \mathbb{R}^n$ using a loop. Test your program for various small vectors. Then, use your program and measure the processing time for vectors of different sizes as

```
system.time(innerproduct(matrix(1,nrow=10000),matrix(1,nrow=10000)))
system.time(innerproduct(matrix(1,nrow=40000),matrix(1,nrow=40000)))
system.time(innerproduct(matrix(1,nrow=160000),matrix(1,nrow=160000)))
system.time(innerproduct(matrix(1,nrow=640000),matrix(1,nrow=640000)))
```

Hence, fill the following table and show that the time complexity of your program is $\mathcal{O}(n)$. Based on your measurements, estimate the time required for the inner product of two vectors of size $n = 640,000,000$.

n	Processing time (seconds)	Increase rate
10,000		–
40,000		
160,000		
640,000		

2. Using your time measurement for $n = 640,000$ in Question 1, estimate how many floating-point operations can be performed per second, assuming that a summation and multiplication is one floating-point operation. This will give a rough idea on how powerful the computer that you employ your program on.

3. Write a program that multiplies a matrix $A \in \mathbb{R}^{m \times n}$ with a vector $x \in \mathbb{R}^n$. Test your program for various small matrices and vectors. Then, use your program and measure the processing time for matrices and vectors of different sizes as

```
system.time(matvecmult(matrix(1,nrow=100,ncol=100),matrix(1,nrow=100)))
system.time(matvecmult(matrix(1,nrow=200,ncol=200),matrix(1,nrow=200)))
system.time(matvecmult(matrix(1,nrow=400,ncol=400),matrix(1,nrow=400)))
system.time(matvecmult(matrix(1,nrow=800,ncol=800),matrix(1,nrow=800)))
```

Hence, fill the following table and show that the time complexity of your program is $\mathcal{O}(n^2)$.

n	Processing time (seconds)	Increase rate
100		–
200		
400		
800		

4. Write a program that multiplies two matrices $A \in \mathbb{R}^{m \times n}$ and $B \in \mathbb{R}^{n \times p}$. Test your program for various small matrices. Then, use your program and measure the processing time for 50×50 and 100×100 matrices as

```
A=matrix(1,nrow=50,ncol=50)
B=matrix(1,nrow=50,ncol=50)
system.time(matmatmult(A,B))
A=matrix(1,nrow=100,ncol=100)
B=matrix(1,nrow=100,ncol=100)
system.time(matmatmult(A,B))
```

Show that your measurements fit into the theoretical complexity, i.e., $\mathcal{O}(n^3)$.

5. Write a recursive program that lists all words with n letters containing "a" and "b". Test your program for $n = 4$, $n = 5$, and $n = 6$. Then, use your program and measure the processing time for larger values of n as

```
system.time(generateab(10))
system.time(generateab(11))
system.time(generateab(12))
system.time(generateab(13))
system.time(generateab(14))
system.time(generateab(15))
```

Hence, fill the following table and show that the time complexity of your program has an exponential order.

n	Processing time (seconds)	Increase rate
10		–
11		
12		
13		
14		
15		

Based on your measurements, estimate the time required for generating and listing all words with $n = 30$ letters.

6. Write a program that calculates the ith Fibonacci number using a loop. Test your code for $i = 10$, $i = 20$, $i = 30$, $i = 40$. How the processing time changes when i gets larger, especially compared to the recursive program that you implemented before? Also find the 1000th Fibonacci number using your program, displaying it approximately.

7. Write a program that calculates the binomial coefficients using the Pascal triangle. The inputs should be the indices of the coefficient, i.e., i and j in

$$b(i, j) = \binom{i}{j} = \frac{i!}{j!(i - j)!}.$$

Measure the time required to find the binomial coefficients $b(16, 8)$, $b(18, 9)$, $b(20, 10)$, and $b(22, 11)$. For these cases, where $j = i/2$, how quickly does the time increase with respect to i?

8. Write a program that calculates the binomial coefficients using the improved recursive formula

$$b(i, j) = \frac{i}{j} b(i - 1, j - 1).$$

Measure the time required to find various binomial coefficients. How fast your program is, especially compared to the program using the Pascal triangle?

Accuracy Issues

5

When comparing programs and algorithms, both two aspects, i.e., efficiency and accuracy, should be considered together. In many cases, accuracy is not critical, such as when outputs are not numeric or they are simply integers. However, it becomes an important issue to assess the accuracy of results when a program contains numerical computations involving real numbers leading to rounding errors. In some cases, rounding errors tend to accumulate and/or be amplified, leading to significantly inaccurate outputs. This short chapter presents some of these interesting cases, along with short discussions of well-known techniques to avoid such accuracy problems.

5.1 Evaluating Mathematical Functions at Difficult Points

Consider the mathematical function

$$f(x) = \frac{1 - \cos x}{x^2}$$

defined for $x \in \mathbb{R}$. First, let us write an R program to plot this function in any given range $x \in [x_{min}, x_{max}]$ by sampling at $n + 1$ points.

```
R Program: Evaluate f(x) = (1-cos x)/x^2 (Original)

01 evaluatefunction1 = function(xmin,xmax,n){
02     x = c(0)
03     f = c(0)
05     for (i in (0:n)){
06         x[i+1] = xmin + i*(xmax-xmin)/n
07         f[i+1] = (1-cos(x[i+1]))/(x[i+1])^2
08     }
09     plot(x,f,type="l",col="blue",xlab="x",ylab="function")
10 }
```

Using this program for $x_{min} = -1$, $x_{max} = 1$, and $n = 100$ as

```
evaluatefunction1(-1,1,100)
```

Ö. Ergül, *Guide to Programming and Algorithms Using R*,
DOI 10.1007/978-1-4471-5328-3_5,
© Springer-Verlag London 2013

Fig. 5.1 Plot of the function $f(x) = (1 - \cos x)/x^2$ in the $[-1, 1]$ range

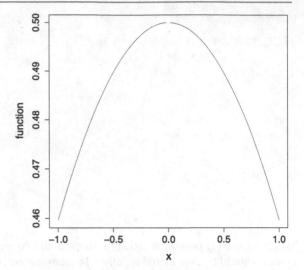

generates the plot depicted in Fig. 5.1. Note that using the built-in `curve` function of R (without writing any program) as

```
curve((1-cos(x))/(x)^2,from=-1,to=1)
```

would generate a similar plot. In any case, the plot seems fine, except at around $x = 0$, where the line is discontinuous. Note that the mathematical function is in fact continuous everywhere, including $x = 0$ with the value of

$$\lim_{x \to 0} \left(\frac{1 - \cos x}{x^2} \right) = \frac{1}{2}.$$

Unfortunately, the evaluation of the function at around $x = 0$ is problematic using the floating-point arithmetic.

To further investigate the behavior of the function at around $x = 0$, we can use the program above as

```
evaluatefunction1(-10^-7,10^-7,200)
```

to generate the zoomed plot depicted in Fig. 5.2. In addition to a persistent discontinuity at $x = 0$, other accuracy problems are clearly visible in this plot. Specifically, the value of the function in this range should be close to 0.5, but we observe incorrect values oscillating between 0 and 1.

The discontinuities in Figs. 5.1 and 5.2 are due to the fact that $(1 - \cos x) = 0$ and $x^2 = 0$ for $x = 0$. Therefore, as the function is evaluated at $x = 0$, we have $0/0$ that leads to a not-a-number (NaN) in R. On the other hand, the accuracy problems that become visible when evaluating the function $f(x) = (1 - \cos x)/x^2$ at around $x = 0$ are due to rounding errors. When x is close to 0, $\cos x$ is close to 1 and $(1 - \cos x)$ is close to zero. Unfortunately, when this subtraction, i.e., one minus $\cos x$, is performed using floating-point arithmetic, it contains rounding errors. This is because the exact representation of $1 - \cos x$ requires more digits (possibly infinite

Fig. 5.2 Plot of the function $f(x) = (1 - \cos x)/x^2$ in the $[-10^{-7}, 10^{-7}]$ range

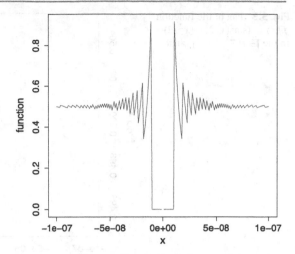

numbers of digits) after the decimal point than allowed on the computer, and hence, some of the "insignificant" digits have to be omitted. The resulting rounding errors are small, but they are amplified as the result of the subtraction is divided by x^2, which is also small when x is close to 0. Note that this term (x^2) also contains rounding errors itself. Consequently, rounding errors significantly contaminate the numerical value of the function when x is small.

Rounding errors often affect the evaluation of functions at critical points. Different strategies can be used to avoid such errors. If possible, the expression of the given function should be replaced with a more stable one via analytical manipulations. Using the identity

$$\cos x = 1 - 2\sin^2(x/2)$$

for the function above, we have

$$f(x) = \frac{1 - \cos x}{x^2} = \frac{1 - (1 - 2\sin^2(x/2))}{x^2} = \frac{2\sin^2(x/2)}{x^2} = \left(\frac{\sin^2(x/2)}{x^2/2}\right),$$

which is much more stable than the original one since it does not contain any difficult subtraction. It only contains a small value divided by another small value, but there is no any amplification of rounding errors to generate significantly incorrect results at the end. Considering this, the following R program can be written:

```
R Program: Evaluate f(x) = (sin^2(x/2))/(x^2/2) (Original)

01 evaluatefunction2 = function(xmin,xmax,n){
02     x = c(0)
03     f = c(0)
05     for (i in (0:n)){
06         x[i+1] = xmin + i*(xmax-xmin)/n
07         f[i+1] = (sin(x[i+1]/2))^2/((x[i+1])^2/2)
08     }
09     plot(x,f,type="l",col="blue",xlab="x",ylab="function")
10 }
```

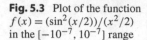

Fig. 5.3 Plot of the function $f(x) = (\sin^2(x/2))/(x^2/2)$ in the $[-10^{-7}, 10^{-7}]$ range

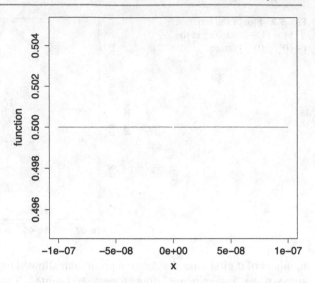

Figure 5.3 depicts a revised plot in the $[-10^{-7}, 10^{-7}]$ range. It can be observed that large oscillations due to rounding errors disappear using the new expression. This plot confirms the improved stability of the modified expression of the function, as described above.

In Fig. 5.3, the discontinuity at $x = 0$ is still visible because, even using the improved formula, we still have 0/0. In fact, this case occurs whenever x^2 is less than the smallest positive floating-point number that can be represented. So, the problem is not limited to a "single" point. In order to handle these cases, it is useful to divide the evaluation of the function into different parts. Specifically, for very small or zero values of x, one can use $f(x) = 1/2$, which is the limit value of the function. Along this direction, the program can be revised as follows:

R Program: Evaluate f(x) = (sin^2(x/2))/(x^2/2) With Check (Original)

```
01 evaluatefunction2withcheck = function(xmin,xmax,n,epsilon){
02     x = c(0)
03     f = c(0)
04     for (i in (0:n)){
05         x[i+1] = xmin + i*(xmax-xmin)/n
06         if (abs(x[i+1]) > epsilon){
07             f[i+1] = (sin(x[i+1]/2))^2/((x[i+1])^2/2)
08         }
09         else{
10             f[i+1] = 1/2
11         }
12     }
13     plot(x,f,type="l",col="blue",xlab="x",ylab="function")
14 }
```

Fig. 5.4 Plot of the function
$f(x) = (\sin^2(x/2))/(x^2/2)$
in the $[-10^{-7}, 10^{-7}]$ range
using a check around $1/2$

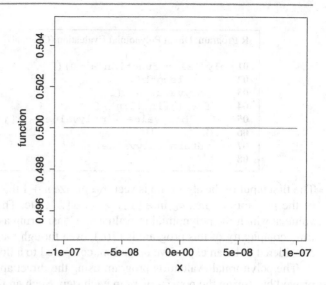

In this program, `epsilon` is an input to control the evaluation of the function. Specifically, when x is in the range $[-\epsilon, \epsilon]$ for a small number ϵ, the value of the function is set to $1/2$ without attempting to evaluate the formula. Using this program as

```
evaluatefunction2withcheck(-10^-7,10^-7,200,10^-10)
```

generates the plot in Fig. 5.4, where no problem is visible at around the critical point.

5.2 Polynomial Evaluation

Polynomials are finite expressions involving constants, variables, and their powers (with nonnegative integer exponents) combined with basic operations, i.e., addition, subtraction, multiplication, and division. In this book, we consider polynomials with a single variable x that can be written in the form of

$$p(x) = \sum_{i=0}^{n} a_i x^i = a_0 + a_1 x + a_2 x^2 + \cdots + a_n x^n,$$

where a_i for $i = 0, 1, \ldots, n$ are constants (coefficients). This polynomial has a degree of n, which is simply the largest exponent. In general, a polynomial of degree n has $n + 1$ terms, but one or some of its coefficients can be zero.

Given a polynomial $p(x)$, it may be desired to compute its value at $x = x_0$, which is called polynomial evaluation. A direct way to do this is just inserting the value of x_0 into the polynomial expression. Such a direct program can be written as follows:

R Program: Direct Polynomial Evaluation (Original)

```
01 polyeval = function(a,x0){
02    n = length(a) - 1
03    polyvalue = a[1]
04    for (j in (1:n)){
05       polyvalue = polyvalue + a[j+1]*(x0)^j
06    }
07    return(polyvalue)
08 }
```

The first input of the algorithm is vector a of size $n + 1$ that includes the coefficients of the polynomial, i.e., a_0 in a[1], a_1 in a[2], etc. The second input x0 is the value at which the polynomial is evaluated. Considering a critical line (line 05), the time complexity of this program is $\mathcal{O}(n)$, even though the power (x0)^j is often considered to be an expensive operation, compared to a floating-point operation.

The polynomial evaluation program using the direct approach can easily be improved by storing the powers of x_0 in each step. Such an improved program can be written as follows:

R Program: Improved Direct Polynomial Evaluation (Original)

```
01 polyevalimproved = function(a,x0){
02    n = length(a) - 1
03    polyvalue = a[1]
04    powersofx0 = 1
05    for (j in (1:n)){
06       powersofx0 = x0*powersofx0
07       polyvalue = polyvalue + a[j+1]*powersofx0
08    }
09    return(polyvalue)
10 }
```

In this program, the powers of x_0 are stored in a variable powersofx0, which is updated and used for each term of the polynomial. It is often assumed that the improved program is faster than the original one since it does not contain any power operation. Nevertheless, a single line (line 05 in the original program) is replaced with two new lines (lines 06 and 07 in the improved program), which may actually increase the processing time depending on the computer. For reducing the processing time, one may consider the Horner's algorithm, as detailed in the next subsection.

5.2.1 Horner's Algorithm

The Horner's algorithm is an efficient method for polynomial evaluation. It is based on rewriting a polynomial

$$p(x) = a_0 + a_1 x + a_2 x^2 + \cdots + a_n x^n$$

as follows. First, we note that

$$p(x) = p_0 = a_0 + xp_1(x),$$

where $p_1(x) = a_1 + a_2x + \cdots + a_nx^{n-1}$ is a polynomial of order $n - 1$. Similarly,

$$p_1(x) = a_1 + xp_2(x),$$

where $p_2(x) = a_2 + a_3x + \cdots + a_nx^{n-2}$. This way, we define a sequence of polynomials

$$p_j(x) = a_j + xp_{j+1}(x)$$

for $j = 0, 1, \ldots, n$ and $p_{n+1}(x) = 0$.

Now, assume that we would like to evaluate the polynomial at $x = x_0$. Considering the sequence of polynomials as defined above, we have

$$y_n = a_n$$
$$y_{n-1} = a_{n-1} + x_0 y_n$$
$$y_{n-2} = a_{n-2} + x_0 y_{n-1}$$
$$\vdots$$
$$y_j = a_j + x_0 y_{j+1}$$
$$\vdots$$
$$y_1 = a_1 + x_0 y_2$$
$$y_0 = a_0 + x_0 y_1,$$

where $y_0 = p_0(x_0) = p(x_0)$. Note that we trace the polynomial in reverse order, i.e., from n to 0. This sequence of evaluations has a recursive structure, but it is commonly implemented via a loop, as in the following program:

```
R Program: Polynomial Evaluation With Horner's Algorithm (Original)

01 polyevalhorner = function(a,x0){
02     n = length(a) - 1
03     polyvalue = a[n+1]
04     for (j in (1:n)){
05         polyvalue = a[n+1-j] + x0*polyvalue
06     }
07     return(polyvalue)
08 }
```

Similar to the previous ones, the time complexity of this program is $\mathcal{O}(n)$. Hence, the order is the same (linear) for all polynomial evaluation programs. On the other hand, the program using the Horner's algorithm contains a single line inside the loop and no power operation, so that it is expected to be faster than the direct evaluation programs. Considering the operations inside the loops, such a speedup in the processing time is limited to two, whereas smaller speedup values are usually observed in practical cases due to fixed lines, such as the for statement, in all programs.

5.2.2   Accuracy of Polynomial Evaluation

Polynomial evaluation programs usually encounter accuracy problems when the value of the polynomial is close to zero. This is similar to the evaluation of functions at critical points, where rounding errors are responsible for inaccurate results. As an example, consider the evaluation of $p(x) = (x - 2)^{10}$ at $x = 2.01$. This polynomial can be rewritten as

$$p(x) = 1024 - 5120x + 11520x^2 - 15360x^3 + 13440x^4 - 8064x^5$$
$$+ 3360x^6 - 960x^7 + 180x^8 - 20x^9 + x^{10}.$$

Then, using our programs as

```
a=c(1024,-5120,11520,-15360,13440,-8064,3360,-960,180,-20,1)
polyeval(a,2.01)
polyevalimproved(a,2.01)
polyevalhorner(a,2.01)
```

we obtain inconsistent results, i.e.,

$$3.683454e-11$$
$$-7.048584e-12$$
$$-2.182787e-11$$

In fact, all these results are incorrect, since $p(2.01) = (2.01 - 2)^{10} = 10^{-20}$. Obviously, using the polynomial evaluation programs, rounding errors become significant as large numbers are added and subtracted to obtain a small result. Even though all final results are small (around 10^{-11}) and close to zero, they may be amplified if these results are to be used somewhere else. Using the factored form, i.e., $p(x) = (x - 2)^{10}$, however, we simply take the power of a small number, which is reliable and less prone to rounding errors.

As a further example, we consider the evaluation of a simple polynomial, i.e.,

$$p(x) = (x - 1)^3 = x^3 - 3x^2 + 3x - 1,$$

at around $x = 1$. In order to evaluate the polynomial at multiple points using the Horner's algorithm, the following program can be used:

```
R Program: Using Horner's Algorithm At Multiple Points (Original)

01 polyevalhornermultiple = function(a,xmin,xmax,n){
02     x = c(0)
03     y = c(0)
04     for (i in (0:n)){
05         x[i+1] = xmin + i*(xmax-xmin)/n
06         y[i+1] = polyevalhorner(a,x[i+1])
07     }
08     plot(x,y,type="l",col="blue",xlab="x",ylab="function")
09 }
```

Fig. 5.5 Plot of the polynomial $p(x) = (x-1)^3 = x^3 - 3x^2 + 3x - 1$ in the [0.99999, 1.00001] range when it is evaluated by using the Horner's algorithm (oscillatory) and the factored form (smooth)

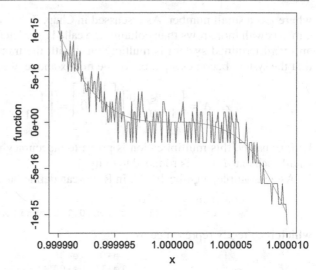

In the above, the program `polyevalhorner` is used as a function at n points in the range $[x_{min}, x_{max}]$, which are indicated by the inputs xmin, xmax, and n. The polynomial coefficients are again provided by an input vector a. Using the program above as

```
polyevalhornermultiple(c(1,-3,3,-1),0.99999,1.00001,200)
```

one may obtain the oscillatory curve depicted in Fig. 5.5. The correct values of the polynomial are also plotted using the factored form $p(x) = (x-1)^3$, leading to the smooth curve in the same figure. We observe that the Horner's algorithm suffers from rounding errors that are clearly visible at around the critical point $x = 1$, where the value of the polynomial is close to zero.

5.3 Matrix–Matrix Multiplications

Up to now, we have seen various cases where rounding errors may significantly affect numerical outputs. In these cases, where functions and polynomials are evaluated at critical points, large numbers are added or subtracted from each other to generate small values. These small values may also be amplified, e.g., via divisions by other small quantities, leading to very inaccurate outputs. In this section, we consider similar effects of rounding errors in matrix operations, where these errors even change the characteristics of the resulting matrices.

Consider the 3×2 matrix

$$A = \begin{bmatrix} 1 & 1 \\ \epsilon & 0 \\ 0 & \epsilon \end{bmatrix},$$

where ϵ is a small number. As discussed in Chap. 7, linear systems involving such a matrix with more rows than columns are called overdetermined. One way to solve an overdetermined system is multiplying it with the transpose of the matrix such that the system becomes square. For the matrix above, we have

$$A^T A = \begin{bmatrix} 1 & \epsilon & 0 \\ 1 & 0 & \epsilon \end{bmatrix} \begin{bmatrix} 1 & 1 \\ \epsilon & 0 \\ 0 & \epsilon \end{bmatrix} = \begin{bmatrix} 1 + \epsilon^2 & 1 \\ 1 & 1 + \epsilon^2 \end{bmatrix}.$$

Unfortunately, this multiplication is prone to inaccuracy problems when ϵ is very small such that $1 + \epsilon^2$ is rounded to unity.

As an example, let ϵ be 10^{-10}. In R, we can define the matrix as

```
epsilon = 10^-10
A = matrix(c(1,epsilon,0,1,0,epsilon),nrow=3)
```

which is correctly represented as

```
1e+00 1e+00
1e-10 0e+00
0e+00 1e-10
```

Then, we can multiply the matrix with its transpose using the built-in functions t (for transpose) and %*% (for matrix–matrix multiplication) as

```
B = t(A)%*%A
```

But, the result of the multiplication, i.e., B, is represented in R as

```
1 1
1 1
```

where ϵ^2 is lost (i.e., rounded to zero), and $1 + \epsilon^2$ is rounded to unity. This is a very serious problem since the matrix involving only ones is rank deficient and the resulting system does not have a unique solution. This type of rounding errors are commonly encountered in matrix operations, which can be interpreted as loss of information considering that matrices usually represent some underlying phenomena in physical life. Similar to the previous examples, a remedy is to modify the solution algorithm, e.g., using factorization methods to solve overdetermined systems rather than matrix–matrix multiplications.

Finally, consider the inner product of two vectors, i.e.,

$$v = \begin{bmatrix} 1 \\ \epsilon \\ -1 \end{bmatrix} \quad \text{and} \quad w = \begin{bmatrix} 1 \\ \epsilon \\ 1 \end{bmatrix},$$

which is equal to ϵ^2. Again, if ϵ is small, the result is prone to disastrous effects of rounding errors. For example, using

```
epsilon = 10^-10
v = c(1,epsilon,-1)
w = c(1,epsilon,1)
t(v)%*%w
```

we obtain zero in R. Similar to the previous example, ϵ^2 is rounded to zero.

5.4   Conclusions

Rounding errors become important when a program contains numerical computations involving real numbers. Errors are introduced as numbers are rounded using floating-point arithmetic. These errors are small, but they may accumulate and/or be amplified, so that outputs may become significantly inaccurate. As shown in this chapter, evaluations of functions and polynomials are prone to stability problems at some critical points. Similarly, matrix–matrix multiplications are interesting examples where rounding errors may change the overall characteristics of output matrices. In Chapter 7, we discuss pivoting as an important tool to avoid rounding errors arising in elimination and factorization methods for linear systems of equations.

5.5   Exercises

1. Consider the following simple example to demonstrate rounding errors. Choose a sufficiently small number, e.g., $\epsilon = 10^{-20}$. Try the following in the R workspace:

```
epsilon = 10^-20
epsilon+1-1
epsilon+(1-1)
```

Explain why the result is different for the second and third lines.

2. This exercise shows how an analytical manipulation may improve the evaluation of a function at around a critical point. Consider the function

$$f(x) = \frac{\exp(2x) - 1}{\exp(x) - 1}.$$

Plot the function in the $x \in [-1, 1]$ range using the built-in function of R as

```
curve((exp(2*x)-1)/(exp(x)-1),from=-1,to=1)
```

to see the problem at $x = 0$. Then, try

```
curve((exp(2*x)-1)/(exp(x)-1),from=-10^-7,to=10^-7)
```

to see inaccuracy problems around this critical point. Then, manipulate the function by factorizing the numerator as

$$\exp(2x) - 1 = (\exp(x) - 1)(\exp(x) + 1)$$

followed by a cancellation. Show that the revised formula behaves well around $x = 0$.

3. This exercise shows how handling special cases may improve the evaluation of a function around a critical point. Write a program called evaluatefunctionsinc

that plots the sinc function

$$f(x) = \frac{\sin x}{x}$$

in a desired range $x \in [x_{min}, x_{max}]$ using a total of n samples. The inputs of the program should be xmin, xmax, and n. Use your function as

```
evaluatefunctionsinc(-10,10,100)
```

to observe the discontinuity at $x = 0$. Also try

```
evaluatefunctionsinc(-10^-20,10^-20,100)
```

to see that the discontinuity problem persists at $x = 0$. Then, modify your program by adding an extra input epsilon such that the limit value of the function, i.e.,

$$\lim_{x \to 0} f(x) = 1,$$

is used in a given narrow range $x \in [-\epsilon, \epsilon]$. Use your revised program as

```
evaluatefunctionsincwithcheck(-10^-20,10^-20,100,10^-30)
```

to observe that the inaccuracy problem at $x = 0$ is solved.

4. Write an R program that evaluates a given polynomial at a desired point directly. (Use the improved version given in this chapter). Use your program to evaluate

$$p(x) = -8 + x + 2x^2 - 6x^3 + 4x^4 + 5x^5 + x^6$$

at $x = -2$.

5. Write an R program that evaluates a given polynomial at a desired point using the Horner's algorithm. Use your program to evaluate

$$p(x) = -8 + x + 2x^2 - 6x^3 + 4x^4 + 5x^5 + x^6$$

at $x = -2$.

6. Describe how the Horner's algorithm works when a polynomial is to be evaluate at $x_0 = 0$. Suggest a modification in the original program to handle this special case more efficiently.

Sorting

6

Sorting is a very important concept in computer science. Given a vector of numbers, the aim is to reorder the elements so that they appear in accordance with a desired rule, i.e., increasing or decreasing order. There are extremely many applications where sorted vectors are required for efficiency. It is also essential to sort the elements efficiently, and it is not surprising that diverse algorithms and their implementations have been (and still being) proposed in the literature for this purpose. Among many of them, in this chapter, we focus on three algorithms, namely, the bubble sort algorithm, the insertion sort algorithm, and the quick sort algorithm. The bubble sort algorithm is one of the most trivial algorithms that was analyzed decades ago. The insertion sort algorithm is another simple one, which can be used to sort small vectors efficiently. Although both algorithms are important sorting tools, they are barely alternative to the quick sort algorithm, which has been the most popular sorting algorithm due to its superior efficiency.

In this chapter, we consider three algorithms separately and analyze them in detail. We use these algorithms to sort the elements of vectors in increasing order. When investigating their computational complexity, sorting algorithms are usually tested under various circumstances. Specifically, as opposed to what we do in the previous chapters, we consider a best case, a worst case, and an average case separately for each sorting program/algorithm when estimating its time complexity. For example, in the best case for bubble sort and insertion sort algorithms, we assume that the input vector is already sorted, hence sorting is not actually required. For these algorithms, the worst case occurs when the input vector is reversely sorted, i.e., the elements of the input vector are sorted in the decreasing order. An average-case analysis is usually more tricky, but we use some heuristic approaches and try to understand the programs and algorithms under normal circumstances. For the quick sort algorithm, we use completely different analysis methods since this algorithm has a different structure. As opposed to the time complexity, the memory complexity of a sorting program/algorithm is usually fixed and does not depend on different cases.

Ö. Ergül, *Guide to Programming and Algorithms Using R*,
DOI 10.1007/978-1-4471-5328-3_6,
© Springer-Verlag London 2013

6.1   Bubble Sort Algorithm

The bubble sort algorithm is a straightforward sorting algorithm based on direct comparisons of elements. Let $a \in \mathbb{R}^n$ be a vector of n elements to be sorted. The bubble sort algorithm starts by comparing $a[1]$ and $a[2]$. If $a[1]$ is greater than $a[2]$, then they are swapped. Next, $a[2]$ and $a[3]$ are compared, and swapped if required. When all consecutive elements in the vector are processed, the algorithm starts another step by going back to the first element of the vector. The vector is processed until no change is required in any step.

For a better understanding of the algorithm, consider an example vector $[5, -3, 4, 6, 3, 1]$. Operations and modifications on the vector in different steps of the algorithm can be written as follows.

- Step 1: $[5, -3, 4, 6, 3, 1] \rightarrow [-3, 5, 4, 6, 3, 1] \rightarrow [-3, 4, 5, 6, 3, 1]$
  $\rightarrow [-3, 4, 5, 6, 3, 1] \rightarrow [-3, 4, 5, 3, 6, 1] \rightarrow [-3, 4, 5, 3, 1, 6]$
- Step 2: $[-3, 4, 5, 3, 1, 6] \rightarrow [-3, 4, 5, 3, 1, 6] \rightarrow [-3, 4, 5, 3, 1, 6]$
  $\rightarrow [-3, 4, 3, 5, 1, 6] \rightarrow [-3, 4, 3, 1, 5, 6] \rightarrow [-3, 4, 3, 1, 5, 6]$
- Step 3: $[-3, 4, 3, 1, 5, 6] \rightarrow [-3, 4, 3, 1, 5, 6] \rightarrow [-3, 3, 4, 1, 5, 6]$
  $\rightarrow [-3, 3, 1, 4, 5, 6] \rightarrow [-3, 3, 1, 4, 5, 6] \rightarrow [-3, 3, 1, 4, 5, 6]$
- Step 4: $[-3, 3, 1, 4, 5, 6] \rightarrow [-3, 3, 1, 4, 5, 6] \rightarrow [-3, 1, 3, 4, 5, 6]$
  $\rightarrow [-3, 1, 3, 4, 5, 6] \rightarrow [-3, 1, 3, 4, 5, 6] \rightarrow [-3, 1, 3, 4, 5, 6]$
- Step 5: $[-3, 1, 3, 4, 5, 6] \rightarrow [-3, 1, 3, 4, 5, 6] \rightarrow [-3, 1, 3, 4, 5, 6]$
  $\rightarrow [-3, 1, 3, 4, 5, 6] \rightarrow [-3, 1, 3, 4, 5, 6] \rightarrow [-3, 1, 3, 4, 5, 6]$

Step 5 does not involve any swap operation, and hence it is the last step. At the end of this step, the elements of the vector are sorted as $[-3, 1, 3, 4, 5, 6]$. Figure 6.1 depicts the application of the bubble sort algorithm to this example vector and the elements of the vector at different steps. In this figure, the elements compared are shown as opaque, whereas other elements are transparent. The status of the vector at the end of each step is also shown.

The bubble sort algorithm is so inefficient that it is not even mentioned in most of the computer science courses. As we will see later, even the misplacement of a single element in an almost sorted vector leads to $\mathcal{O}(n^2)$ time complexity using the bubble sort algorithm. The problem lies in the fact that any unsorted vector needs to be traced for $\mathcal{O}(n)$ times (so there are $\mathcal{O}(n)$ steps), whereas each step requires $\mathcal{O}(n)$ comparisons, leading to the quadratic overall complexity of the algorithm. In other words, the bubble sort algorithm requires a total of $\mathcal{O}(n^2)$ comparisons between n elements, unless the given vector is already sorted. Along this direction, a more efficient sorting algorithm should have a lower number of comparisons with a reduced number of steps or number of comparisons per step or both.

Following the discussion above, the bubble sort algorithm can be implemented as follows:

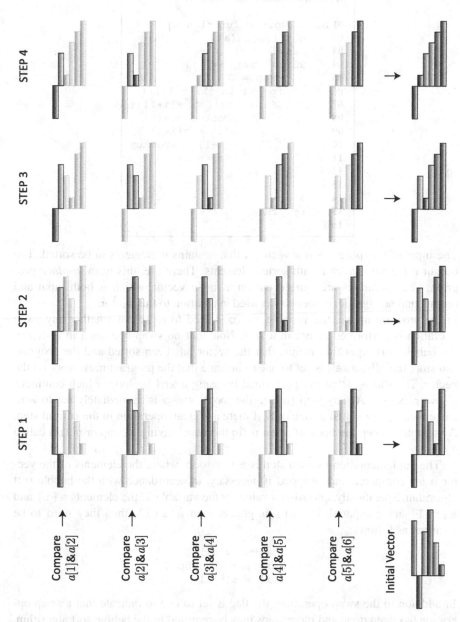

Fig. 6.1 Application of the bubble sort algorithm to a vector [5, −3, 4, 6, 3, 1] and the steps that require swap operations

```
R Program: Bubble Sort (Original)

01 bubblesort = function(a){
02     n = length(a)
03     swap = 1
04     while (swap == 1){
05         swap = 0
06         for (i in (1:(n-1))){
07             if (a[i] > a[i+1]){
08                 abackup = a[i]
09                 a[i] = a[i+1]
10                 a[i+1] = abackup
11                 swap = 1
12             }
13         }
14     }
15     return(a)
16 }
```

The input of this program is a vector a that contains *n* elements to be sorted. The output is the same vector with sorted elements. Therefore, this is an *in-place* program, i.e., operations are carried out on a single vector, which is both input and output, and no significant memory is used in addition to this vector.

In the program above, the variable swap is used to represent whether any swap operation is performed or not in a step. Note that no swap operation in a step of the bubble sort algorithm means that the vector has been sorted and the program can stop. Initially, swap is set to one to indicate that the program must work on the vector. The sorting steps are performed by using a while loop, which continues if swap is one. At any step (inside the loop), swap is immediately set to zero since it can be switched to one only if there is a swap operation in the current step. A variable to keep the track of a status (in this case, having a swap or not) is called a *flag*.

The implementation of each step is a for loop, where the elements of the vector a are compared and swapped if necessary, in accordance with the bubble sort algorithm. Specifically, choosing a value for the variable i, the elements a[i] and a[i+1] are compared. If a[i] is greater than a[i+1], then they need to be swapped as follows:

```
abackup = a[i]
a[i+1] = abackup
a[i] = a[i+1]
```

In addition to the swap operation, the flag is set to one to indicate that a swap operation has been done and more steps may be required in the bubble sort algorithm. Note that we are using a backup variable abackup to facilitate the swap operations. Having said this, the following would be incorrect:

```
a[i+1] = a[i]
a[i] = a[i+1]
```

Using this pair of lines, both `a[i]` and `a[i+1]` would be the same at the end, whereas the original `a[i+1]` is completely lost.

The bubble sort program above can easily be improved with the following observation. The largest element is located at the last position and it does not move after the first step. In other words, it is "locked." Hence, one does not need to check and compare `a[n-1]` and `a[n]` after the first step since they should not require a swap later. Similarly, the second largest element is located in the correct position, i.e., at the $(n-1)$th position, and does not move after the second step, etc. Based on these, some unnecessary checks can be avoided, leading to the following improved program:

```
R Program: Improved Bubble Sort (Original)

01 bubblesortimproved = function(a){
02    n = length(a)
03    swap = 1
04    step = 1
05    while (swap == 1){
06       swap = 0
07       if (step < n){
08          for (i in (1:(n-step))){
09             if (a[i] > a[i+1]){
10                abackup = a[i]
11                a[i] = a[i+1]
12                a[i+1] = abackup
13                swap = 1
14             }
15          }
16       }
17       step = step + 1
18    }
19    return(a)
20 }
```

In the `for` loop of this program, `i` changes from 1 to `n-step` rather than 1 to `n-1`. Here, the variable `step` is the index of the step, which is initially set to one and incremented at the end of each step as

$$step = step + 1$$

This way, unnecessary comparisons described above are easily avoided.

Now, let us calculate the cost of the improved bubble sort program. The memory complexity of the program is $\mathcal{O}(n)$ considering the input vector a. On the other hand, the time complexity depends on the elements of the input vector, and we need consider each case separately.

- Best Case: In the best case, i.e., when the vector is already sorted, only one step is performed, and no swap is required. In this case, lines 09–13 can be considered as critical lines, which are executed for $n-1$ times since the value of `step` is one. Therefore, $T_{\text{all}}^{\text{best}} = \mathcal{O}(n)$.

- Worst Case: In the worst case, i.e., when the vector is reversely sorted, $n - 1$ steps are required, whereas each comparison requires a swap. Then, the critical lines 09–13 are executed from 1 to n-step, where step changes from 1 to $n - 1$. Therefore, we have

$$T_{\text{all}}^{\text{worst}} = C \sum_{s=1}^{n-1} (n - s) = C \sum_{s'=1}^{n-1} s' = C \frac{n(n-1)}{2} = \mathcal{O}(n^2),$$

where C is a constant.

- Almost the Best Case: In order to understand the performance of the improved bubble sort program under normal circumstances, we consider almost the best case, where the initial vector is correctly sorted except the smallest element. Let the smallest element be located at the last (nth) position instead of the first position. Then, there should be again $n - 1$ steps, even though each step involves only a single swap operation. Hence, in this case, lines 10–13 are executed once per step, but line 09 is executed from 1 to n-step (as in the worst case), becoming a critical line. Therefore, we have

$$T_{\text{all}}^{\text{almost-best}} = C \sum_{s=1}^{n-1} (n - s) = \mathcal{O}(n^2),$$

where C is a constant. Even though the sorting is significantly faster compared to the worst case (because lines 10–13 are executed once per step), the time complexity is still $\mathcal{O}(n^2)$.

- Average Case: The improved bubble sort program requires $\mathcal{O}(n^2)$ processing time, even when a single element is misplaced in the initially sorted vector. This also means that, except for the best case, i.e., when the entire vector is already sorted, the improved bubble sort program has $\mathcal{O}(n^2)$ time complexity, including all average cases. Therefore,

$$T_{\text{all}}^{\text{average}} = \mathcal{O}(n^2).$$

Due to its relatively high time complexity, the bubble sort algorithm is rarely used in real-life applications. In the next subsections, we consider the insertion sort and quick sort algorithms that are more efficient and used in practice.

6.2 Insertion Sort Algorithm

The insertion sort is another simple algorithm, which is based on direct comparisons of elements. Let a be a vector of n elements to be sorted. The insertion sort algorithm starts by comparing $a[2]$ with $a[1]$ and swapping them if required. This operation is exactly the same as the first operation of the bubble sort algorithm. But then, $a[3]$ is compared with both $a[2]$ and $a[1]$ to make sure that it is inserted in the correct position. The algorithm continues by inserting $a[4]$, $a[5]$, etc., in the correct positions considering the elements with smaller indices that are already sorted. Hence, as opposed to the bubble sort algorithm, the vector is traced only once, but each element (except $a[2]$) is compared with more than one element to be inserted in the correct position.

Let us apply the insertion sort to the example vector $a = [5, -3, 4, 6, 3, 1]$.

- Insertion of $a[2]$: $[5, -3, 4, 6, 3, 1] \rightarrow [-3, 5, 4, 6, 3, 1]$
- Insertion of $a[3]$: $[-3, 5, 4, 6, 3, 1] \rightarrow [-3, 4, 5, 6, 3, 1] \rightarrow [-3, 4, 5, 6, 3, 1]$
- Insertion of $a[4]$: $[-3, 4, 5, 6, 3, 1] \rightarrow [-3, 4, 5, 6, 3, 1]$
- Insertion of $a[5]$: $[-3, 4, 5, 6, 3, 1] \rightarrow [-3, 4, 5, 3, 6, 1] \rightarrow [-3, 4, 3, 5, 6, 1]$
  $\rightarrow [-3, 3, 4, 5, 6, 1] \rightarrow [-3, 3, 4, 5, 6, 1]$
- Insertion of $a[6]$: $[-3, 3, 4, 5, 6, 1] \rightarrow [-3, 3, 4, 5, 1, 6] \rightarrow [-3, 3, 4, 1, 5, 6]$
  $\rightarrow [-3, 3, 1, 4, 5, 6] \rightarrow [-3, 1, 3, 4, 5, 6]$
  $\rightarrow [-3, 1, 3, 4, 5, 6]$

Figure 6.2 illustrates the elements of the example vector in different steps of the insertion sort algorithm. Theoretically, the insertion of $a[i]$ should require $(i - 1)$ comparisons, but as shown in this example (i.e., insertion of $a[4]$), further comparisons can be avoided if a comparison does not require a swap. In other words, the number of comparisons depends on the values of the elements that are already sorted, as well as the element to be inserted.

The advantage of the insertion sort algorithm over the bubble sort algorithm may not be obvious without a detailed analysis. For a vector of n elements, there should be a total of $n - 1$ insertions (can be considered as steps), while each insertion requires $\mathcal{O}(n)$ comparisons in average. In fact, as presented below, the average-case time complexity of the insertion sort algorithm is $\mathcal{O}(n^2)$, similar to that of the bubble sort algorithm. Nevertheless, the insertion sort algorithm becomes very efficient for nearly sorted vectors, which require several comparisons per step, leading to a linear overall complexity.

Based on the discussion above, the insertion sort algorithm can be implemented as follows:

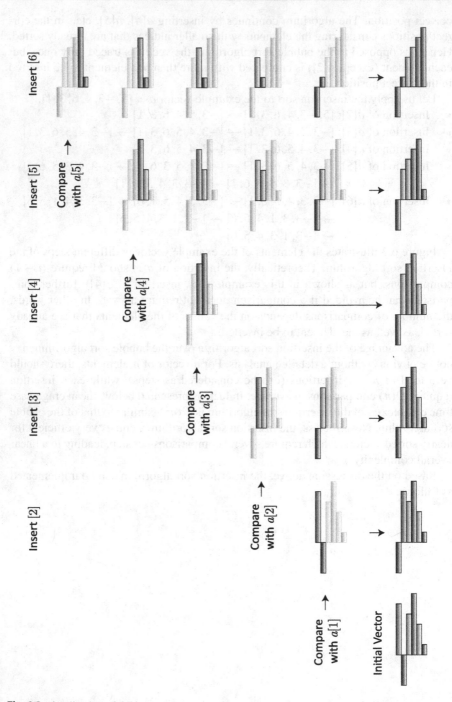

Fig. 6.2 Application of the insertion sort algorithm to the vector [5, −3, 4, 6, 3, 1]

```
R Program: Insertion Sort (Original)

01 insertionsort = function(a){
02    n = length(a)
03    for (i in (2:n)){
04       for (j in (1:(i-1))){
05          if (a[i-j] > a[i-j+1]){
06             abackup = a[i-j]
07             a[i-j] = a[i-j+1]
08             a[i-j+1] = abackup
09          }
10          else{
11             break
12          }
13       }
14    }
15    return(a)
16 }
```

The input/output of this program is again a vector a, which contains n elements. In the program, the outer loop is constructed for the insertion steps with the variable i changing from 2 to n. Choosing a value for i and the element to be inserted (initially at the ith position), maximum i-1 comparisons are required. Therefore, in the inner loop, the variable j changes from 1 to i-1. Comparisons are executed in line 05 as

$$\text{if } (a[i-j] > a[i-j+1]) \{$$

Note that the element to be inserted may move in each comparison, and hence comparisons are made between $(i - j)$th and $(i - j + 1)$th elements above. In any comparison, if the element a[i-j] is greater than the element a[i-j+1], they are swapped. Otherwise, the break command in line 11 is executed, which immediately ends the inner loop. This is essential to avoid unnecessary comparisons. Because, if a[i-j] is not greater than a[i-j+1], the element to be inserted, which is now located at $(i - j + 1)$th position, is already in the correct place, and it should not move any further.

The memory complexity of the insertion sort program above is $\mathcal{O}(n)$ and it is an in-place program. For the time complexity, we again consider different cases.

- Best Case: In the best case, i.e., when the vector is already sorted, the if statement

$$a[i-j] > a[i-j+1]$$

never holds. Hence, the inner for loop is broken immediately when j is one. Considering line 05 as a critical line, which is executed for $(n - 1)$ times due to the outer loop, we have

$$T_{\text{all}}^{\text{best}} = \mathcal{O}(n).$$

- Worst case: In the worst case, i.e., when the vector is reversely sorted, the conditional statement `[i-j] > a[i-j+1]` always holds, and each comparison requires a swap. In other words, `break` is never executed. In this case, lines 05–08 can be considered to be critical to derive the time complexity as

$$T_{\text{all}}^{\text{worst}} = C \sum_{i=2}^{n} (i-1) = C \sum_{i'=1}^{n-1} i' = C \frac{n(n-1)}{2} = \mathcal{O}(n^2),$$

where C is a constant. In the above, the summation represents the outer loop, whereas $i - 1$ is the cost due to the inner loop for a given i.

- Almost the Best Case: Consider almost the best case, where the initial vector is correctly sorted except the smallest element, which is located at the last (nth) position. This means that, for the elements from `a[2]` to `a[n-1]`, the inner loop is immediately broken. For these elements, line 05 is critical, which is executed for $(n - 1)$ times. On the contrary, for the last element, i.e., `a[n]`, `break` is never executed. For this element, lines 05–08 are critical, which are executed for $(n - 1)$ times since `j` changes from 1 to `i-1` when the value of `i` is n. Considering all contributions, we have

$$T_{\text{all}}^{\text{almost-best}} = C(n-1) + D(n-1) = \mathcal{O}(n),$$

where C and D are constants. Obviously, for this case, the insertion sort algorithm is more efficient than the bubble sort algorithm.

- Average Case: We do not have a quick conclusion for the average time complexity of the insertion sort program/algorithm since it has $\mathcal{O}(n)$ complexity for almost the best case. In order to analyze the program in an average case, consider the inner loop

```
for (j in (1:(i-1))){
```

running from 1 to `i-1` with a possible break. In the best case, this loop always breaks whenever `j` is 1 since any element to be inserted is already located in the correct position. In the worst case, however, the loop always continues without any break from 1 to `i-1` since all elements to be inserted should move to the first position. Then, in an average case, we can assume that the loop continues up to approximately half of `i` and then breaks. Hence, the time complexity can be written as

$$T_{\text{all}}^{\text{average}} = C \sum_{i=2}^{n} (i/2 - 1) = \mathcal{O}(n^2),$$

which means that we again have a quadratic order in average.

As a result, the insertion sort algorithm performs well for almost sorted vectors, but its time complexity is $\mathcal{O}(n^2)$ in average cases. Due to this high time complexity, the insertion sort algorithm is rarely used, only when the input vector is small and/or nearly sorted.

Fig. 6.3 Application of the
quick sort algorithm to the
vector $[5, -3, 4, 6, 3, 1]$

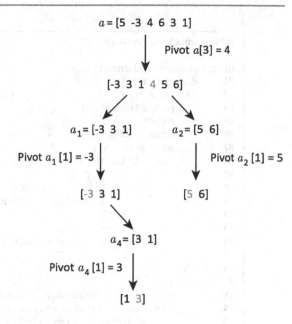

6.3   Quick Sort

The quick sort algorithm is a well-known and popular method, which is commonly used in many applications. Its popularity is due to its lower time complexity, which is $\mathcal{O}(n \log n)$ in average.

Let a be a vector of n elements to be sorted. The quick sort algorithm starts by choosing a pivot element a[p]. The vector is reordered so that all elements smaller than a[p] have smaller indices and all elements larger than a[p] have larger indices. After this reordering, the pivot is in its correct position (say, at a[r]), but this is not necessarily true for the other elements. Then, the quick sort algorithm continues recursively by considering the smaller vectors a[1:r-1] and a[r+1:n] and applying the same operations on them.

Consider the application of the quick sort algorithm to an example vector involving six elements, e.g., $a = [5, -3, 4, 6, 3, 1]$. As a rule to choose the pivot, we can use $p = \lfloor n/2 \rfloor$, where $\lfloor \cdot \rfloor$ represents the floor operation. Then, the algorithm works as depicted in Fig. 6.3. Note that as the recursion continues, vectors with one element arise, and no further sorting is required for them. This condition, i.e., having one element, can be considered as the termination condition for the recursion.

The quick sort algorithm with the pivoting strategy $p = \lfloor n/2 \rfloor$ can be implemented as follows:

R Program: Quick Sort (Original)

```
01 quicksort = function(a){
02     n = length(a)
03     if (n > 1){
04         p = floor(n/2)
05         pivot = a[p]
06         asmaller = c()
07         alarger = c()
08         for (i in (1:n)){
09             if (i != p){
10                 if (a[i] <= pivot){
11                     asmaller = rbind(asmaller,a[i])
12                 }
13                 else{
14                     alarger = rbind(a[i],alarger)
15                 }
16             }
17         }
18         asmaller = quicksort(asmaller)
19         alarger = quicksort(alarger)
20         a = rbind(asmaller,a[p],alarger)
21     }
22     return(a)
23 }
```

This program is not in-place since we allocate two new vectors, namely, `asmaller` and `alarger`, to collect the elements that are smaller and larger, respectively, than the pivot. Then, the memory requirement can be written as

$$M_{\text{all}}(n) = C + nD + M_{\text{all}}(n_s) + M_{\text{all}}(n_l),$$

where C and D are constants. In the above, n_s and n_l represent the numbers of elements in `asmaller` and `alarger` vectors, respectively. Therefore, $n_s + n_l = (n - 1)$, but their values depend on the input vector.

Now let us consider the worst-case scenario for the program above. As opposed to the other sorting programs and algorithms, the worst case of the quick sort program/algorithm is not the case where the input vector is reversely sorted. Instead, the value of the pivot compared to the other elements is the critical factor. Specifically, the worst case happens when the pivot is either the smallest or the largest element by "coincidence." Considering the latter, all elements other than the pivot are collected in `asmaller`, whereas `alarger` has no element. In other words, $n_s = n - 1$, $n_l = 0$, and

$$M_{\text{all}}(n) = C + nD + M_{\text{all}}(n - 1).$$

Assuming that this worst-case selection occurs in all steps of the recursion, we have

$$M_{\text{all}}^{\text{worst}}(n) = C + nD + M_{\text{all}}^{\text{worst}}(n - 1),$$

which can be solved to arrive at

$$M_{\text{all}}^{\text{worst}}(n) = \mathcal{O}(n^2)$$

as the worst-case memory requirement.

For the quick sort algorithm, the best case happens when the value of the pivot is perfect such that nearly half of the elements are smaller than the pivot. Consequently, $n_s = \lfloor n/2 \rfloor - 1$, $n_l = n - \lfloor n/2 \rfloor$, and

$$M_{\text{all}}(n) = C + nD + M_{\text{all}}(\lfloor n/2 \rfloor - 1) + M_{\text{all}}(n - \lfloor n/2 \rfloor).$$

Assuming that this best-case selection occurs in all steps of the recursion, we obtain

$$M_{\text{all}}^{\text{best}}(n) = \mathcal{O}(n \log n)$$

as the best-case memory requirement.

It should be noted that there are also improved (in-place) implementations of the quick sort algorithm that require only $\mathcal{O}(\log n)$ extra memory other than for the input vector, leading to $M_{\text{all}}^{\text{best}}(n) = \mathcal{O}(n) + \mathcal{O}(\log n) = \mathcal{O}(n)$, but they are out of the scope of this book.

Now, let us investigate the time complexity of the quick sort program in detail.

- Best Case: In the best case, i.e., where pivots are chosen perfectly in all steps, the processing time can be written as

$$T_{\text{all}}^{\text{best}}(n) = C + nD + T_{\text{all}}^{\text{best}}(\lfloor n/2 \rfloor - 1) + T_{\text{all}}^{\text{best}}(n - \lfloor n/2 \rfloor),$$

  leading to

$$T_{\text{all}}^{\text{best}}(n) = \mathcal{O}(n \log n),$$

  similar to the best-case memory.

- Worst case: In the worst case, i.e., where pivots are extremum (minimum or maximum) elements in all steps, the processing time can be written as

$$T_{\text{all}}^{\text{worst}}(n) = C + nD + T_{\text{all}}^{\text{worst}}(n - 1),$$

  leading to

$$T_{\text{all}}^{\text{worst}}(n) = \mathcal{O}(n^2),$$

  similar to the worst-case memory.

- Average case: In general, choosing the best or worst pivot in all steps of the recursion has a very low probability. In the best case, input vectors are divided equally into pairs of vectors. In the worst case, all elements (except the pivots) are collected in one vector. Along this direction, in order to consider different possibilities between the best and worst selections of pivots, one can write

$$T_{\text{all}}^{\text{average}}(n) = C + nD + \frac{1}{\lfloor n/2 \rfloor} \sum_{i=1}^{\lfloor n/2 \rfloor} \left(T_{\text{all}}^{\text{average}}(n - i) + T_{\text{all}}^{\text{average}}(i - 1) \right),$$

where different values of i accounts for different possible splits. A rigorous analysis of this formula leads to

$$T_{all}(n) = \mathcal{O}(n \log n)$$

as the average time complexity of the quick sort program.

To sum up, the time complexity of the quick sort program is $\mathcal{O}(n \log n)$ in average. This low complexity is an important advantage of the quick-sort algorithm over other sorting algorithms in the literature.

As a demonstration, Fig. 6.4 depicts the application of the quick sort program to a vector of 2500 elements. First, we generate a random vector and its plot as

```
v = rnorm(2500,0,10)
plot(v,col="blue",xlab="Index",ylab="Element Values")
```

Then, we apply the quick sort program and plot the resulting vector as

```
w = quicksort(v)
plot(w,col="blue",xlab="Index",ylab="Element Values")
```

It can be observed that the elements are nicely ordered using the quick sort program, verifying its correct implementation.

6.4 Comparisons

Table 6.1 lists the time complexity of the three sorting algorithms considered in this chapter. In the worst-case scenarios, all algorithms have $\mathcal{O}(n^2)$ complexity. In the average cases, however, the quick sort algorithm with $\mathcal{O}(n \log n)$ complexity is more efficient than others. Its low average-time complexity is the reason why the quick sort algorithm is preferred in many real-life applications. If the initial vector is known to be almost sorted, then the insertion sort algorithm (with $\mathcal{O}(n)$ complexity) may be used instead of the quick sort algorithm, but this requires a priori knowledge on the vector, and the gain in the processing time may not be very critical.

When comparing complexities, it is relatively easier to understand polynomial orders. For example, if an algorithm has a quadratic time complexity, increasing the input size twice increases the processing time by $2^2 = 4$ times for large inputs. However, if an algorithm has a logarithmic time complexity, i.e., $\mathcal{O}(\log n)$, it is difficult to estimate the increase in the processing time when the input size is increased, e.g., twice. The ignored base of the logarithm also leads to confusions. For a more correct interpretation, one may consider that the input size is squared (rather than multiplied), which leads to twofold increase in the processing time if the algorithm has a logarithmic complexity.

In order to understand $\mathcal{O}(n \log n)$, consider that n is very large, which is in fact an assumption that is already made for the asymptotic analysis. For a large n, increasing the input size to $2n$ leads to an almost twofold increase in the processing time, since the $\log n$ term contributes a little. This term can add a twofold increase only when the input size is increased to a very large value, i.e., n^2. But, in the case of such a

Fig. 6.4 Application of the quick sort program to a vector of random elements

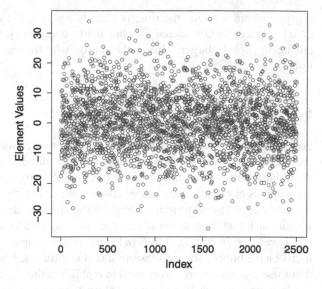

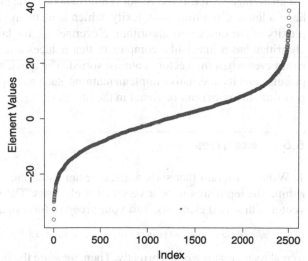

Table 6.1 Comparison of three sorting algorithms in terms of the processing time

Algorithm	Bubble sort	Insertion sort	Quick sort
Worst-Case Scenario	Reversely sorted	Reversely sorted	Worst pivots
Worst Case	$\mathcal{O}(n^2)$	$\mathcal{O}(n^2)$	$\mathcal{O}(n^2)$
Average Case	$\mathcal{O}(n^2)$	$\mathcal{O}(n^2)$	$\mathcal{O}(n \log n)$
Best-Case Scenario	Already sorted	Already sorted	Best pivots
Almost Best Case	$\mathcal{O}(n^2)$	$\mathcal{O}(n)$	$\mathcal{O}(n \log n)$
Best Case	$\mathcal{O}(n)$	$\mathcal{O}(n)$	$\mathcal{O}(n \log n)$

big jump from n to n^2, the time is already squared due to the n term. Therefore, $\mathcal{O}(n \log n)$ can be considered as a linear-like complexity, which behaves like $\mathcal{O}(n)$ but being slightly larger. This is the reason why this expression is usually called linearithmic.

6.5 Conclusions

Sorting is one of the important problems in computer science since sorted vectors are required in many application areas. Given a numeric vector of n elements, it is desirable to sort its elements as fast as possible. Among many of them, the quick sort algorithm is coming forward as an efficient method with $\mathcal{O}(n \log n)$ time complexity in average. This algorithm is based on recursively dividing vectors into smaller vectors such that the number of comparisons required to sort a given vector is drastically reduced from $\mathcal{O}(n^2)$ to $\mathcal{O}(n \log n)$. In this chapter, for comparisons, we also focus on the bubble sort and insertion sort algorithms, but it should be emphasized that these algorithms are rarely used in real life as they have $\mathcal{O}(n^2)$ time complexity for an average vector. If the vector is almost sorted, the insertion sort algorithm may have a linear $\mathcal{O}(n)$ time complexity, which is mathematically better than the complexity of the quick sort algorithm. Nevertheless, for large vectors, the quick sort algorithm has a linear-like complexity that reduces a need for an alternative algorithm even when the vector is almost sorted. The quick sort algorithm is extremely popular, and its alternative implementations (such as in-place, optimized, and using pivoting strategies) can be found in the literature.

6.6 Exercises

1. Write a program that sorts a given vector using the improved bubble sort algorithm. The input should be a vector of n elements. The output should be the same vector with sorted elements. Test your program for a small vector as

```
bubblesortimproved(matrix(c(50,-3,1,6,12,10,0,-40,1,5,8,1),ncol=1))
```

to make sure that it works correctly. Then, measure the time required to sort random vectors of 500, 1000, and 2000 elements as

```
system.time(bubblesortimproved(matrix(rnorm(500,0,1),ncol=1)))
system.time(bubblesortimproved(matrix(rnorm(1000,0,1),ncol=1)))
system.time(bubblesortimproved(matrix(rnorm(2000,0,1),ncol=1)))
```

Investigate the timing results in terms of the time complexity of the program.

2. Write a program that sorts a given vector using the insertion sort algorithm. The input should be a vector of n elements. The output should be the same vector with sorted elements. Test your program for a small vector as

```
insertionsort(matrix(c(50,-3,1,6,12,10,0,-40,1,5,8,1),ncol=1))
```

to make sure that it works correctly. Then, measure the time required to sort random vectors of 500, 1000, and 2000 elements as

```
system.time(insertionsort(matrix(rnorm(500,0,1),ncol=1)))
system.time(insertionsort(matrix(rnorm(1000,0,1),ncol=1)))
system.time(insertionsort(matrix(rnorm(2000,0,1),ncol=1)))
```

Investigate the timing results in terms of the time complexity of the program.

3. Use your insertion sort program to perform the following experiment. First, create a vector of 500 almost-sorted elements as

```
v = insertionsort(matrix(rnorm(500,0,1),ncol=1))
v[500] = -100
```

Note that the last element of the vector is set to -100, which is (most probably) misplaced. Then, measure the time required to sort the vector as

```
system.time(insertionsort(v))
```

Repeat the experiment for vectors of size 1000 and 2000 to investigate the time complexity of the program for almost sorted vectors.

4. Write a program that sorts a given vector using the quick sort algorithm with $p = \lfloor n/2 \rfloor$ pivoting. The input should be a vector of n elements. The output should be the same vector with sorted elements. Test your program for a small vector as

```
quicksort(matrix(c(50,-3,1,6,12,10,0,-40,1,5,8,1),ncol=1))
```

to make sure that it works correctly. Then, measure the time required to sort random vectors of 1000, 2000, 10,000, and 20,000 elements as

```
system.time(quicksort(matrix(rnorm(1000,0,1),ncol=1)))
system.time(quicksort(matrix(rnorm(2000,0,1),ncol=1)))
system.time(quicksort(matrix(rnorm(10000,0,1),ncol=1)))
system.time(quicksort(matrix(rnorm(20000,0,1),ncol=1)))
```

Investigate the timing results in terms of the time complexity of the program.

5. Consider a modified quick sort program/algorithm, where the pivot is selected as the first element of the vector. Describe the disadvantages of the program/algorithm when the input vector is almost sorted.

Solutions of Linear Systems of Equations

7

Linear systems of equations are important components in many basic areas, such as biology, chemistry, computer science, economics, engineering, and physics. Mathematical modeling of real-life scenarios often leads to linear systems of equations, whose solutions are required to understand the underlying phenomena. Solution techniques for linear systems have been developed for decades under the name of linear algebra. It is also common to approximate nonlinear systems with linear ones in order to benefit the advanced methods in this area.

7.1   Overview of Linear Systems of Equations

A linear system of equations is a collection of linear equations involving a set of variables. As an example, consider the linear equation

$$x + 2y = 4$$

involving two variables, i.e., x and y. As depicted in Fig. 7.1, this equation represents a line in the two-dimensional space. Now, consider another equation

$$x - y = 1$$

involving the same variables. This equation corresponds to another line. If we would like to consider the two equations at the same time, we may write it in a matrix equation (linear system) form as

$$\begin{bmatrix} 1 & 2 \\ 1 & -1 \end{bmatrix} \begin{bmatrix} x \\ y \end{bmatrix} = \begin{bmatrix} 4 \\ 1 \end{bmatrix}.$$

The linear system above can be interpreted as "two equations with two unknowns." Solution of such a system is relatively easy by a direct substitution. For example, using the first equation, we have $x = 4 - 2y$, which can be inserted into the second equation to get $4 - 2y - y = 1$ or $-3y = -3$. Hence, $y = 1$ and $x =$

Ö. Ergül, *Guide to Programming and Algorithms Using R*,
DOI 10.1007/978-1-4471-5328-3_7,
© Springer-Verlag London 2013

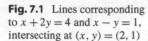

Fig. 7.1 Lines corresponding to $x + 2y = 4$ and $x - y = 1$, intersecting at $(x, y) = (2, 1)$

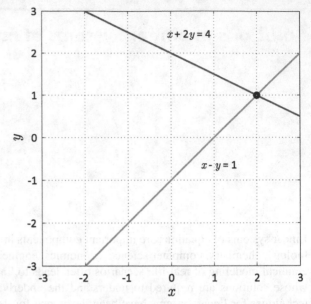

$4 - 2y = 2$. In other words, $(x, y) = (2, 1)$ is the solution to the linear system. As depicted in Fig. 7.1, the solution actually corresponds to the intersection of the two lines describing the two equations.

In general, we have n equations involving n unknowns, where $n > 2$. Such linear systems can be difficult to solve by a direct substitution. Nevertheless, we are able to derive systematic ways and techniques to solve large matrix equations involving large numbers of unknowns. Geometric interpretations of large linear systems can be difficult, but this does not prevent us to solve them by abstracting each equation as an $(n - 1)$-dimensional "line" in the n-dimensional space.

Before going into further details of the solution techniques, it is useful to categorize linear systems of equations to understand them and their possible solutions. Assume that we have m equations involving n unknowns, i.e.,

$$a_{11}x_1 + a_{12}x_2 + \ldots + a_{1n}x_n = b_1,$$
$$a_{21}x_1 + a_{22}x_2 + \ldots + a_{2n}x_n = b_2,$$
$$a_{31}x_1 + a_{32}x_2 + \ldots + a_{3n}x_n = b_3,$$
$$\vdots \quad \vdots \quad \vdots \quad \vdots \quad \ddots \quad \vdots \quad \vdots \quad \vdots \quad \vdots$$
$$a_{m1}x_1 + a_{m2}x_2 + \ldots + a_{mn}x_n = b_m.$$

Then, in the matrix form, we have

$$\begin{bmatrix} a_{11} & a_{12} & \ldots & a_{1n} \\ a_{21} & a_{22} & \ldots & a_{2n} \\ a_{31} & a_{32} & \ldots & a_{3n} \\ \vdots & \vdots & \ddots & \vdots \\ a_{m1} & a_{m2} & \ldots & a_{mn} \end{bmatrix} \begin{bmatrix} x_1 \\ x_2 \\ x_3 \\ \vdots \\ x_n \end{bmatrix} = \begin{bmatrix} b_1 \\ b_2 \\ b_3 \\ \vdots \\ b_m \end{bmatrix}.$$

Depending on the values of m and n, we have three different cases.

(1)   If $m = n$, then the number of equations is equal to the number of unknowns. Such a system is called a square system, considering that the matrix has a square shape with equal numbers of rows and columns.

(2)   If $m > n$, then there are more equations than unknowns. Such a system is called an overdetermined system.

(3)   If $m < n$, then there are more unknowns than equations. Such a system is called an underdetermined system.

In this book, we will mainly consider square systems ($m = n$).

The values of m and n do not give a complete information about the solution. We again have three different cases.

(1)   Unique Solution: A system may have a unique solution. Only square and overdetermined systems may have unique solutions.

(2)   Infinitely Many Solutions: A system may have infinitely many solutions. Such a system can be square, underdetermined, or overdetermined.

(3)   No Solution: A system may have no solution. Such a system can be square, underdetermined, or overdetermined.

Hence, a square system may have a unique solution, infinitely many solutions, or no solution.

Let us now consider various square systems with different properties.

- $$\begin{bmatrix} 1 & 2 \\ 1 & -1 \end{bmatrix} \begin{bmatrix} x \\ y \end{bmatrix} = \begin{bmatrix} 4 \\ 1 \end{bmatrix}$$

  is a square system with a unique solution $(x, y) = (2, 1)$.

- $$\begin{bmatrix} 1 & 2 \\ 2 & 4 \end{bmatrix} \begin{bmatrix} x \\ y \end{bmatrix} = \begin{bmatrix} 4 \\ 8 \end{bmatrix}$$

  is a square system with infinitely many solutions. For example, inserting $x = 4 - 2y$ into second equation, we obtain $2(4 - 2y) + 4y = 8$ or $8 = 8$, which is always correct, independently of the values of x and y. This is because these two equations are linearly dependent, i.e., one of them can be obtained from the other and vice versa. In this example, the second equation is obtained via multiplying the first equation by two. Hence, it does not provide a new information regarding the variables x and y. Geometrically, both equations correspond to the same line in the two-dimensional space. Hence, their intersection is also the same line involving infinitely many points (solutions).

- $$\begin{bmatrix} 1 & 2 \\ 2 & 4 \end{bmatrix} \begin{bmatrix} x \\ y \end{bmatrix} = \begin{bmatrix} 4 \\ 4 \end{bmatrix}$$

  is a square system with no solution. For example, inserting $x = 4 - 2y$ into second equation, we obtain $2(4 - 2y) + 4y = 4$ or $8 = 4$, which is always incorrect for any values of x and y. Geometrically, these equations correspond to two parallel lines in the two-dimensional space. Hence, they do not intersect and there is not any point (solution) that is on the both lines at the same time.

Geometric interpretations of the systems defined above with infinitely many solutions and no solution are illustrated in Fig. 7.2.

Fig. 7.2 Lines corresponding to $x + 2y = 4$, $2x + 4y = 8$, and $2x + 4y = -3$

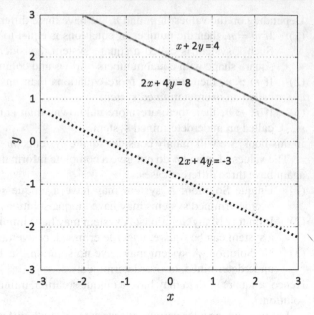

7.2 Solutions of Triangular Systems

Solution of a general $n \times n$ matrix equation involves two main stages.

(1) Modify the matrix equation (using elimination or factorization) such that it becomes easier to solve.

(2) Apply substitution systematically to solve for unknowns.

We first consider the second stage and focus on solution methods for simple matrix equations, namely, triangular systems.

An $n \times n$ lower-triangular matrix

$$L = \begin{bmatrix} l_{11} & 0 & 0 & \dots & 0 \\ l_{21} & l_{22} & 0 & \dots & 0 \\ l_{31} & l_{32} & l_{33} & \dots & 0 \\ \vdots & \vdots & \vdots & \ddots & \vdots \\ l_{n1} & l_{n2} & l_{n3} & \dots & l_{nn} \end{bmatrix}$$

has zero elements above the diagonal, i.e., $L[i, j] = 0$ for $j > i$. An $n \times n$ upper-triangular matrix

$$U = \begin{bmatrix} u_{11} & u_{12} & u_{13} & \dots & u_{1n} \\ 0 & u_{22} & u_{23} & \dots & u_{2n} \\ 0 & 0 & u_{33} & \dots & u_{3n} \\ \vdots & \vdots & \vdots & \ddots & \vdots \\ 0 & 0 & 0 & \dots & u_{nn} \end{bmatrix}$$

has zero elements below the diagonal, i.e., $U[i, j] = 0$ for $i > j$. A matrix, which is both lower and upper triangular, is called diagonal since such a matrix may have nonzero elements only on the diagonal, i.e.,

$$D = \begin{bmatrix} d_{11} & 0 & 0 & \cdots & 0 \\ 0 & d_{22} & 0 & \cdots & 0 \\ 0 & 0 & d_{33} & \cdots & 0 \\ \vdots & \vdots & \vdots & \ddots & \vdots \\ 0 & 0 & 0 & \cdots & d_{nn} \end{bmatrix}.$$

Matrix equations involving diagonal matrices are trivial to solve. For example, if

$$D \begin{bmatrix} x_1 \\ x_2 \\ x_3 \\ \vdots \\ x_n \end{bmatrix} = \begin{bmatrix} b_1 \\ b_2 \\ b_3 \\ \vdots \\ b_n \end{bmatrix},$$

one can find that

$$\begin{bmatrix} x_1 \\ x_2 \\ x_3 \\ \vdots \\ x_n \end{bmatrix} = \begin{bmatrix} b_1/d_{11} \\ b_2/d_{22} \\ b_3/d_{33} \\ \vdots \\ b_n/d_{nn} \end{bmatrix}.$$

Matrix equations involving lower-triangular and upper-triangular matrices can be solved via forward and backward substitutions, respectively.

7.2.1 Forward Substitution

Consider a matrix equation involving an $n \times n$ lower-triangular matrix, i.e.,

$$\begin{bmatrix} l_{11} & 0 & 0 & \cdots & 0 \\ l_{21} & l_{22} & 0 & \cdots & 0 \\ l_{31} & l_{32} & l_{33} & \cdots & 0 \\ \vdots & \vdots & \vdots & \ddots & \vdots \\ l_{n1} & l_{n2} & l_{n3} & \cdots & l_{nn} \end{bmatrix} \begin{bmatrix} x_1 \\ x_2 \\ x_3 \\ \vdots \\ x_n \end{bmatrix} = \begin{bmatrix} b_1 \\ b_2 \\ b_3 \\ \vdots \\ b_n \end{bmatrix}.$$

The first equation can be written as

$$l_{11}x_1 + 0x_2 + 0x_3 + \cdots + 0x_n = b_1$$

or

$$l_{11}x_1 = b_1,$$

leading to

$$x_1 = b_1/l_{11}.$$

In other words, the first equation can be solved without using the other equations. Let us consider the second equation now. Omitting the multiplications with zeros, we have

$$l_{21}x_1 + l_{22}x_2 = b_2$$

or

$$x_2 = (b_2 - x_1 l_{21})/l_{22}.$$

Obviously, the value of x_2 depends on the value of x_1. Also note that the value of x_1 is found above and already available for the calculation of x_2. Similarly, using the third equation, we get

$$x_3 = (b_3 - x_1 l_{31} - x_2 l_{32})/l_{33},$$

where x_1 and x_2 are available and can be used to find x_3. In general,

$$x_i = (b_i - x_1 l_{i1} - x_2 l_{i2} - \cdots - x_{(i-1)} l_{i(i-1)})/l_{ii}$$

for $3 < i \le n$. Based on these, one can write the following program for the forward substitution:

R Program: Forward Substitution (Original)

```
01 forwardsub = function(L,b){
02     x = c(0)
03     n = nrow(L)
04     for (i in (1:n)){
05         x[i] = b[i]
06         if (i > 1){
07             for (j in (1:(i-1))){
08                 x[i] = x[i] - L[i,j]*x[j]
09             }
10         }
11         x[i] = x[i]/L[i,i]
12     }
13     return(cbind(x))
14 }
```

Note that we use cbind to return the solution as a column vector.

The time complexity of the program above can easily be found by noting that line 08 is a critical line. This line is executed for

$$\sum_{i=2}^{n} (i-1) = \sum_{i'=1}^{n-1} i' = \frac{n(n-1)}{2} = n^2/2 - n/2$$

times, leading to $\mathcal{O}(n^2)$ time complexity. In the above, the summation accounts for the outer loop (where the loop variable i changes from 1 to n, while line 08 is not executed when i equals 1), and $i - 1$ stands for the number of executions for a given i due to the inner loop. The memory complexity of the forward substitution program is also $\mathcal{O}(n^2)$, considering the storage of the matrix L.

7.2.2 Backward Substitution

Consider a matrix equation involving an $n \times n$ upper-triangular matrix, i.e.,

$$
\begin{bmatrix}
u_{11} & u_{12} & u_{13} & \cdots & u_{1n} \\
0 & u_{22} & u_{23} & \cdots & u_{2n} \\
0 & 0 & u_{33} & \cdots & u_{3n} \\
\vdots & \vdots & \vdots & \ddots & \vdots \\
0 & 0 & 0 & \cdots & u_{nn}
\end{bmatrix}
\begin{bmatrix}
x_1 \\ x_2 \\ x_3 \\ \vdots \\ x_n
\end{bmatrix}
=
\begin{bmatrix}
b_1 \\ b_2 \\ b_3 \\ \vdots \\ b_n
\end{bmatrix}.
$$

The last (nth) equation can be written as

$$ u_{nn} x_n = b_n, $$

leading to

$$ x_n = b_n / u_{nn}. $$

In other words, the last equation can be solved without using the other equations. Finding the value of x_n, one can consider the $(n-1)$th equation to compute $x_{(n-1)}$ as

$$ x_{(n-1)} = \left(b_{(n-1)} - x_n u_{(n-1)n}\right)/u_{(n-1)(n-1)}. $$

Similarly,

$$ x_{(n-2)} = \left(b_{(n-2)} - x_{(n-1)} u_{(n-2)(n-1)} - x_n u_{(n-2)n}\right)/u_{(n-2)(n-2)}. $$

In general,

$$ x_i = \left(b_i - x_{(i+1)} u_{i(i+1)} - x_{(i+2)} u_{i(i+2)} - \cdots - x_n u_{i,n}\right)/u_{ii} $$

for $1 \leq i < (n-2)$. Note that the procedure is very similar to the forward substitution, but we only process the matrix in the backward direction from the last row to the first row. Such an algorithm can be implemented as follows:

```
R Program: Backward Substitution (Original)

01 backwardsub = function(U,b){
02     x = c(0)
03     n = nrow(U)
04     for (i in (n:1)){
05         x[i] = b[i]
06         if (i < n){
07             for (j in ((i+1):n)){
08                 x[i] = x[i] - U[i,j]*x[j]
09             }
10         }
11         x[i] = x[i]/U[i,i]
12     }
13     return(cbind(x))
14 }
```

In the program above, note that the index of outer loop, i.e.,

```
for (i in (n:1)){
```

changes in a reverse order from n to 1. Line 08 is again a critical line and is executed for $n^2/2 - n/2$ times, leading to $\mathcal{O}(n^2)$ time complexity.

Both forward and backward substitution methods fail when one of the diagonal elements of the matrix is zero. This is due to the fact that such a matrix is *singular*, and in fact, the underlying linear system does not have any solution. An attempt of substitution to such a system leads to a divide-by-zero error, leading to infinite elements in the solution vector.

7.3   Gaussian Elimination

Triangular systems are easy to solve using forward and backward substitutions. Unfortunately, most of the systems derived in real-life applications involve nontriangular matrices, whose solutions require more than substitution. For those systems, one can apply the Gaussian elimination to modify the matrix equation so that the matrix becomes upper triangular (alternatively lower triangular).

7.3.1   Elementary Row Operations

The Gaussian elimination is based on two types of elementary row operations, i.e., replacement and permutation. Consider the ith and jth rows of an $n \times n$ matrix A, where $i \neq j$.

- Replacement: Replace the ith row with a combination of the ith and jth rows, i.e.,

$$A[i,:] + \alpha A[j,:] \to A[i,:].$$

- Permutation: Swap the ith and jth rows, i.e.,

$$A[i, :] \leftrightarrow A[j, :].$$

Replacement can be sufficient to convert a general matrix into an upper-triangular form. Permutation is required for pivoting, as described later. In any case, all operations that are applied to the matrix should also be applied to the right-hand-side vector for consistency. This is particularly required to avoid changing the solution by elementary row operations. A systematic technique to apply same operations to a matrix and a right-hand-side vector is to combine (augment) them before elimination.

As an example, consider the following 3×3 matrix equation $Ax = b$:

$$\begin{bmatrix} 2 & 1 & -2 \\ 3 & -1 & 4 \\ 1 & -2 & 2 \end{bmatrix} \begin{bmatrix} x_1 \\ x_2 \\ x_3 \end{bmatrix} = \begin{bmatrix} 1 \\ 11 \\ 6 \end{bmatrix}.$$

Before applying replacement operations, we augment the matrix and the right-hand-side vector as

$$\{A|b\} = \begin{bmatrix} 2 & 1 & -2 & | & 1 \\ 3 & -1 & 4 & | & 11 \\ 1 & -2 & 2 & | & 6 \end{bmatrix}.$$

Next, we eliminate the elements in the first column below the diagonal, i.e., $A[2, 1] = 3$ and $A[3, 1] = 1$, using $A[1, 1] = 2$. In order to eliminate $A[2, 1]$, we can multiply the first row with $3/2$ and subtract it from the second row. This can be written as

$$\{A|b\}[2, :] - (3/2)\{A|b\}[1, :] \rightarrow \{A|b\}[2, :]$$

leading to

$$\begin{bmatrix} 2 & 1 & -2 & | & 1 \\ 3 & -1 & 4 & | & 11 \\ 1 & -2 & 2 & | & 6 \end{bmatrix} \rightarrow \begin{bmatrix} 2 & 1 & -2 & | & 1 \\ 0 & -5/2 & 7 & | & 19/2 \\ 1 & -2 & 2 & | & 6 \end{bmatrix}.$$

As a result of the replacement operation, $A[2, 1]$ becomes zero. But, note that, the other elements in the same row, including $b[2]$, are also modified for consistency.

In order to eliminate $A[3, 1]$ using $A[1, 1]$, we multiply the first row with $1/2$ and subtract it from the third row, i.e.,

$$\{A|b\}[3, :] - (1/2)\{A|b\}[1, :] \rightarrow \{A|b\}[3, :],$$

leading to

$$\begin{bmatrix} 2 & 1 & -2 & | & 1 \\ 0 & -5/2 & 7 & | & 19/2 \\ 1 & -2 & 2 & | & 6 \end{bmatrix} \rightarrow \begin{bmatrix} 2 & 1 & -2 & | & 1 \\ 0 & -5/2 & 7 & | & 19/2 \\ 0 & -5/2 & 3 & | & 11/2 \end{bmatrix}.$$

At this stage, all elements in the first column, except $A[1, 1]$, are zero. Hence, the matrix becomes "similar" to an upper-triangular matrix. However, we should continue and eliminate all terms below the diagonal. Specifically, we should now consider the second column and eliminate $A[3, 2]$. On the other hand, we cannot use $A[1, 2]$ for this purpose. Because such a replacement operation involving the first row would create a nonzero element at $A[3, 1]$ and ruin our previous efforts. A better strategy is to use $A[2, 2]$ to eliminate $A[3, 2]$ with the replacement operation

$$\{A|b\}[3, :] - \{A|b\}[2, :] \to \{A|b\}[3, :].$$

This leads to

$$\begin{bmatrix} 2 & 1 & -2 & | & 1 \\ 0 & -5/2 & 7 & | & 19/2 \\ 0 & -5/2 & 3 & | & 11/2 \end{bmatrix} \to \begin{bmatrix} 2 & 1 & -2 & | & 1 \\ 0 & -5/2 & 7 & | & 19/2 \\ 0 & 0 & -4 & | & -4 \end{bmatrix}.$$

The final expression can be rewritten as a matrix equation, i.e.,

$$\begin{bmatrix} 2 & 1 & -2 \\ 0 & -5/2 & 7 \\ 0 & 0 & -4 \end{bmatrix} \begin{bmatrix} x_1 \\ x_2 \\ x_3 \end{bmatrix} = \begin{bmatrix} 1 \\ 19/2 \\ -4 \end{bmatrix},$$

where the matrix is now upper triangular. Note that the matrix equation changes but the system does not change by elementary row operations. In fact, we still consider the same system with the same solution. The final matrix equation can be solved via a backward substitution, and we obtain the solution as

$$\begin{bmatrix} x_1 \\ x_2 \\ x_3 \end{bmatrix} = \begin{bmatrix} 2 \\ -1 \\ 1 \end{bmatrix}.$$

Note that this solution satisfies both the triangular matrix equation and the original matrix equation.

7.3.2   Steps of the Gaussian Elimination

Consider a general $n \times n$ matrix equation $Ax = b$, i.e.,

$$\begin{bmatrix} a_{11} & a_{12} & a_{13} & \cdots & a_{1n} \\ a_{21} & a_{22} & a_{23} & \cdots & a_{2n} \\ a_{31} & a_{32} & a_{33} & \cdots & a_{3n} \\ \vdots & \vdots & \vdots & \ddots & \vdots \\ a_{n1} & a_{n2} & a_{n3} & \cdots & a_{nn} \end{bmatrix} \begin{bmatrix} x_1 \\ x_2 \\ x_3 \\ \vdots \\ x_n \end{bmatrix} = \begin{bmatrix} b_1 \\ b_2 \\ b_3 \\ \vdots \\ b_n \end{bmatrix}.$$

Steps of the Gaussian elimination can be listed as follows.
- Step 0: Augment the matrix and the right-hand-side vector, i.e., form $\{A|b\}$.
- Step 1: Eliminate the elements in the first column using the first row.

– Eliminate a_{21} using a_{11}.

$$\{A|b\}[2,:] - m_{21}\{A|b\}[1,:] \rightarrow \{A|b\}[2,:] \quad (m_{21} = a_{21}/a_{11})$$

– Eliminate a_{31} using a_{11}.

$$\{A|b\}[3,:] - m_{31}\{A|b\}[1,:] \rightarrow \{A|b\}[3,:] \quad (m_{31} = a_{31}/a_{11})$$

– ...

– Eliminate a_{n1} using a_{11}.

$$\{A|b\}[n,:] - m_{n1}\{A|b\}[1,:] \rightarrow \{A|b\}[n,:] \quad (m_{n1} = a_{n1}/a_{11})$$

• Step 2: Eliminate the elements in the second column using the second row.
  – Eliminate a_{32} using a_{22}.

$$\{A|b\}[3,:] - m_{32}\{A|b\}[2,:] \rightarrow \{A|b\}[3,:] \quad (m_{32} = a_{32}/a_{22})$$

  – Eliminate a_{42} using a_{22}.

$$\{A|b\}[4,:] - m_{42}\{A|b\}[2,:] \rightarrow \{A|b\}[4,:] \quad (m_{42} = a_{42}/a_{22})$$

  – ...

  – Eliminate a_{n2} using a_{22}.

$$\{A|b\}[n,:] - m_{n2}\{A|b\}[2,:] \rightarrow \{A|b\}[n,:] \quad (m_{n2} = a_{n2}/a_{22})$$

• ...
• Step k: Eliminate the elements in the kth column using the kth row.
• ...
• Step $(n-1)$: Eliminate the elements in the $(n-1)$th column using the $(n-1)$th row.

The operations listed above should be performed consecutively by considering the fact that the matrix elements are updated at each step. We also note that each elimination operation involves a multiplier $m_{ik} = a_{ik}/a_{kk}$ for $k < i \leq n$. Following the Gaussian elimination described above, the system becomes upper triangular that can be solved via a backward substitution.

7.3.3 Implementation

Based on the steps described above, we are now ready to implement the Gaussian elimination algorithm:

```
R Program: Gaussian Elimination (Original)

01 gaussianelimination = function(Ab){
02     n = nrow(Ab)
03     for (k in (1:(n-1))){
04         for (i in ((k+1):n)){
05             mik = Ab[i,k]/Ab[k,k]
06             Ab[i,k] = 0
07             for (j in ((k+1):(n+1))){
08                 Ab[i,j] = Ab[i,j] - mik*Ab[k,j]
09             }
10         }
11     }
12     return(Ab)
13 }
```

In the program above, the input is an $n \times (n + 1)$ matrix Ab that includes the combination (augmentation) of the $n \times n$ matrix and the right-hand-side vector. The output is the same matrix, including an $n \times n$ upper-triangular matrix and the modified right-hand-side vector. For the time complexity of the program, we note that line 08 is a critical line. This line is inside three loops and executed for a total of

$$\sum_{k=1}^{n-1} (n - k)(n - k + 1)$$

times. Inserting $k' = n - k$ above, we have

$$\sum_{k=1}^{n-1} (n - k)(n - k + 1) = \sum_{k'=1}^{n-1} k'(k' + 1) = \sum_{k'=1}^{n-1} (k')^2 + \sum_{k'=1}^{n-1} k'$$

$$= \frac{n(n - 1)(2n - 1)}{6} + \frac{n(n - 1)}{2}.$$

Therefore, the time complexity of the Gaussian elimination program/algorithm is $\mathcal{O}(n^3)$. Despite this cubic time complexity, the memory complexity of the Gaussian elimination is $\mathcal{O}(n^2)$, considering the storage for the matrix Ab.

7.4   LU Factorization

The Gaussian elimination is an important technique for the solution of matrix equations. Another popular technique is the LU factorization, which is based on the decomposition of matrices into lower-triangular (L) and upper-triangular (U) parts, i.e.,

$$A = LU.$$

Consider a matrix equation $Ax = b$ involving a square matrix A. Inserting the LU factorization of the matrix (after it is found), we obtain

$$LUx = b,$$

which can be rewritten as

$$Ly = b,$$

where

$$Ux = y.$$

Hence, if the LU factorization of a matrix can be found, then the solution of the related system requires only a forward substitution (to solve $Ly = b$), followed by a backward substitution (to solve $Ux = y$).

LU factorization is directly related to the Gaussian elimination. Specifically, the Gaussian elimination can be considered as a process to convert the initial matrix into an upper-triangular one, i.e.,

$$A \to U.$$

The resulting matrix U can be chosen as the upper-triangular matrix in the LU factorization. Then, it can be shown that

$$L = \begin{bmatrix} 1 & 0 & 0 & \cdots & 0 \\ m_{21} & 1 & 0 & \cdots & 0 \\ m_{31} & m_{32} & 1 & \cdots & 0 \\ \vdots & \vdots & \vdots & \ddots & \vdots \\ m_{n1} & m_{n2} & m_{n3} & \cdots & 1 \end{bmatrix}.$$

Specifically, the corresponding lower-triangular matrix L consists of the multipliers m_{ik} (for $k < i \leq n$) used during the Gaussian elimination and ones on the diagonal.

Based on the discussion above, a program for the LU factorization can be written as follows. Note the similarities between this program and the Gaussian elimination program.

R Program: LU Factorization (Original)

```
01 lufactorization = function(A){
02     n = nrow(A)
03     L = matrix(0,nrow=n,ncol=n)
04     for (k in (1:(n-1))){
05        for (i in ((k+1):n)){
06           L[i,k] = A[i,k]/A[k,k]
07           A[i,k] = 0
08           for (j in ((k+1):n)){
09              A[i,j] = A[i,j] - L[i,k]*Ab[k,j]
10           }
11        }
12     }
13     for (k in (1:n)){
14        L[k,k] = 1
15     }
16     return(cbind(L,A))
17 }
```

In this program, the input is an $n \times n$ matrix A to be factorized. The output is an $n \times 2n$ matrix containing the lower-triangular and upper-triangular matrices of the factorization. Similar to the Gaussian elimination, the time and memory complexities of the LU factorization are $\mathcal{O}(n^3)$ and $\mathcal{O}(n^2)$, respectively.

Although the LU factorization is directly related to the Gaussian elimination, there is a distinct advantage of the LU factorization when multiple right-hand-side vectors are involved in the solution of a problem. In many real-life applications, a set of linear systems involving the same matrix but different right-hand-side vectors is derived. Using the Gaussian elimination, each linear system should be solved separately. Using the LU factorization, however, only one factorization is sufficient. Following the factorization, forward and backward substitutions can be performed efficiently (with $\mathcal{O}(n^2)$ complexity) for each right-hand-side vector.

Consider again a 3×3 matrix equation $Ax = b$,

$$\begin{bmatrix} 2 & 1 & -2 \\ 3 & -1 & 4 \\ 1 & -2 & 2 \end{bmatrix} \begin{bmatrix} x_1 \\ x_2 \\ x_3 \end{bmatrix} = \begin{bmatrix} 1 \\ 11 \\ 6 \end{bmatrix}.$$

As shown before, matrix A can be converted into an upper triangular matrix via a Gaussian elimination, i.e.,

$$A \rightarrow \begin{bmatrix} 2 & 1 & -2 \\ 0 & -5/2 & 7 \\ 0 & 0 & -4 \end{bmatrix},$$

using the multipliers $m_{21} = 3/2$, $m_{31} = 1/2$, and $m_{32} = 1$. Hence, the LU factorization of A can be written as

$$
\begin{bmatrix} 2 & 1 & -2 \\ 3 & -1 & 4 \\ 1 & -2 & 2 \end{bmatrix} = \begin{bmatrix} 1 & 0 & 0 \\ 3/2 & 1 & 0 \\ 1/2 & 1 & 1 \end{bmatrix} \begin{bmatrix} 2 & 1 & -2 \\ 0 & -5/2 & 7 \\ 0 & 0 & -4 \end{bmatrix}.
$$

Following this factorization, we need to apply the forward and backward substitutions to solve the system. First, consider the forward substitution for the lower-triangular system

$$
\begin{bmatrix} 1 & 0 & 0 \\ 3/2 & 1 & 0 \\ 1/2 & 1 & 1 \end{bmatrix} \begin{bmatrix} y_1 \\ y_2 \\ y_3 \end{bmatrix} = \begin{bmatrix} 1 \\ 11 \\ 6 \end{bmatrix},
$$

which leads to

$$
\begin{bmatrix} y_1 \\ y_2 \\ y_3 \end{bmatrix} = \begin{bmatrix} 1 \\ 19/2 \\ -4 \end{bmatrix}.
$$

Using this result, we apply the backward substitution for the upper-triangular system

$$
\begin{bmatrix} 2 & 1 & -2 \\ 0 & -5/2 & 7 \\ 0 & 0 & -4 \end{bmatrix} \begin{bmatrix} x_1 \\ x_2 \\ x_3 \end{bmatrix} = \begin{bmatrix} 1 \\ 19/2 \\ -4 \end{bmatrix},
$$

leading to

$$
\begin{bmatrix} x_1 \\ x_2 \\ x_3 \end{bmatrix} = \begin{bmatrix} 2 \\ -1 \\ 1 \end{bmatrix}
$$

as the solution of the overall system.

We underline that, following the factorization, the factors can be used to solve for any right-hand side vector. For example, consider

$$
b = \begin{bmatrix} -9 \\ 3 \\ 4 \end{bmatrix}.
$$

Applying forward and backward substitutions as described above gives

$$
x = \begin{bmatrix} -2 \\ -1 \\ 2 \end{bmatrix}
$$

as the solution for this right-hand-side vector.

7.5   Pivoting

The Gaussian elimination (hence, the LU factorization) fails when the diagonal element of the matrix at any step is zero. This is because the multiplier

$$mik = Ab[i,k]/Ab[k,k]$$

becomes infinite when $Ab[k,k]$ is zero. On the other hand, this does not mean that the system has no solution. In fact, in most cases, the system does have a solution (if, at the same time, the matrix is not upper or lower triangular). But, the elimination fails just because the diagonal element is zero. In order to solve this issue, a well-known strategy is pivoting. Specifically, the partial pivoting technique can be used to avoid simple failures in the Gaussian elimination.

The Gaussian elimination without pivoting is based on a type of elementary row operations, namely replacement. Another type of elementary row operations, which is the key for the partial pivoting, is permutation. A permutation operation can be described simply as swapping pairs of rows. Note that, when a permutation is applied to the augmented matrix, the solution of the system does not change. Hence, such an operation is allowed anytime during the Gaussian elimination.

The idea in the partial pivoting is as follows. If the diagonal element used in the kth step ($Ab[k,k]$) is zero, then the kth row can be swapped with another row such that the diagonal element becomes nonzero. Along this direction, the row to be swapped should be selected carefully. Specifically, in order to avoid ruining the previous elimination steps, the row to be swapped should be below the kth row. This way, zero elements created in the previous steps remain unchanged, and the elimination can be maintained as desired.

The partial pivoting described above may also be useful to increase the accuracy of the Gaussian elimination. In general, a diagonal element $Ab[k,k]$ can be very small such that the corresponding multipliers mik are large numbers. Note that this may not be possible to detect at the beginning since matrix elements are updated during the elimination and such a small $Ab[k,k]$ can be encountered at any step. Using large multipliers is totally safe if the Gaussian elimination is performed exactly, i.e., without any rounding errors. On computers, however, floating-point representation of numbers can lead to disastrous effects when small diagonal elements are used to generate large multipliers so that rounding errors are amplified. Partial pivoting is useful to avoid these inaccuracies since small diagonal elements (i.e., not only zeros) can be replaced with larger ones by swapping rows appropriately.

Although there can be different strategies for the partial pivoting, we present the most basic one here. Consider the kth step of the elimination. We would like to eliminate the elements in the kth column (below the diagonal element) using the kth row. Before the elimination, we check all elements below the diagonal and find the largest one (called pivot) among them. Then, the kth row is swapped with the pivot row before the elimination operations.

A program for the Gaussian elimination with partial pivoting can be written as follows:

```
R Program: Gaussian Elimination With Partial Pivoting (Original)

01 gaussianeliminationpartial = function(Ab){
02     n = nrow(Ab)
03     for (k in (1:(n-1))){
04         pivotindex = k
05         for (i in ((k+1):n)){
06             if (abs(Ab[i,k]) > abs(Ab[pivotindex,k]))){
07                 pivotindex = i
08             }
09         }
10         if (pivotindex != k){
11             for (j in (k:(n+1))){
12                 buffer = Ab[k,j]
13                 Ab[k,j] = Ab[pivotindex,j]
14                 Ab[pivotindex,j] = buffer
15             }
16         }
17         for (i in ((k+1):n)){
18             mik = Ab[i,k]/Ab[k,k]
19             Ab[i,k] = 0
20             for (j in ((k+1):(n+1))){
21                 Ab[i,j] = Ab[i,j] - mik*Ab[k,j]
22             }
23         }
24     }
25     return(Ab)
26 }
```

This program is the same as the Gaussian elimination program without pivoting, except lines 04–09 (finding the pivot) and lines 10–16 (swapping the rows). Note that, when swapping the rows, j values that represent column indices start from k instead of 1, i.e.,

```
for (j in (k:(n+1))){
```

since the elements from 1 to $k-1$ in the swapped rows are zero due to the previous elimination steps.

Now, let us consider the additional time cost due to the partial pivoting. Considering the worst case, i.e., where swapping is required and the pivot is located in the last row in each step, we have

$$T_{\text{add}} = (n-1)T_{04} + T_{05} \sum_{k=1}^{n-1} (n-k+1) + (T_{06} + T_{07}) \sum_{k=1}^{n-1} (n-k)$$

$$+ (n-1)T_{10} + T_{11} \sum_{k=1}^{n-1} (n-k+3) + (T_{12} + T_{13} + T_{14}) \sum_{k=1}^{n-1} (n-k+2).$$

Evaluating the summations, we obtain

$$T_{\text{add}} = \mathcal{O}(n^2).$$

Consequently, considering the $\mathcal{O}(n^3)$ time complexity of the Gaussian elimination without pivoting, the additional cost due to the partial pivoting is negligible when n is large. In other words, the Gaussian eliminations with and without partial pivoting have almost the same cost for large systems. Therefore, the partial pivoting is commonly used in Gaussian elimination codes since it prevents unnecessary breakdowns due to zero diagonal elements and increases the stability against rounding errors.

The partial pivoting can also be used in the LU factorization. Such a decomposition can be written as

$$PA = L'U',$$

where L' and U' are lower and upper triangular matrices, respectively. Due to the partial pivoting, in general, these matrices are not the same as the matrices L and U satisfying $A = LU$. Because, the effect of swapping rows is represented by a matrix P that premultiplies A so that $A = LU = P^{-1}L'U'$. In this case, P is called the permutation matrix, which involves a single unity element in each row (or each column) other than zeros.

Lets consider again a 3×3 matrix equation $Ax = b$,

$$\begin{bmatrix} 2 & 1 & -2 \\ 3 & -1 & 4 \\ 1 & -2 & 2 \end{bmatrix} \begin{bmatrix} x_1 \\ x_2 \\ x_3 \end{bmatrix} = \begin{bmatrix} 1 \\ 11 \\ 6 \end{bmatrix}.$$

Augmenting the matrix and the right-hand-side vector, we have

$$\{A|b\} = \begin{bmatrix} 2 & 1 & -2 & | & 1 \\ 3 & -1 & 4 & | & 11 \\ 1 & -2 & 2 & | & 6 \end{bmatrix}.$$

Considering the first column of $\{A|b\}$, we note that $A[2, 1] = 3$ is the pivot. Hence, we swap the first and the second rows as

$$\begin{bmatrix} 2 & 1 & -2 & | & 1 \\ 3 & -1 & 4 & | & 11 \\ 1 & -2 & 2 & | & 6 \end{bmatrix} \rightarrow \begin{bmatrix} 3 & -1 & 4 & | & 11 \\ 2 & 1 & -2 & | & 1 \\ 1 & -2 & 2 & | & 6 \end{bmatrix}.$$

Next, we eliminate the elements in the first column below the diagonal. The required replacement operations are

$$\{A|b\}[2, :] - (2/3)\{A|b\}[1, :] \rightarrow \{A|b\}[2, :]$$

and

$$\{A|b\}[3, :] - (1/3)\{A|b\}[1, :] \rightarrow \{A|b\}[3, :],$$

Table 7.1 Processing Times (in seconds) required for applying the Gaussian elimination to matrix equations of various sizes

Matrix size	Without pivoting	With pivoting	Difference
50×50	0.269	0.280	0.011
100×100	2.054	2.171	0.117
200×200	16.990	17.548	0.558

leading to

$$\begin{bmatrix} 3 & -1 & 4 & | & 11 \\ 2 & 1 & -2 & | & 1 \\ 1 & -2 & 2 & | & 6 \end{bmatrix} \rightarrow \begin{bmatrix} 3 & -1 & 4 & | & 11 \\ 0 & 5/3 & -14/3 & | & -19/3 \\ 0 & -5/3 & 2/3 & | & 7/3 \end{bmatrix}.$$

In the next step, the pivot is $A[2, 2] = 5/3$ since $|A[2, 2]| = |A[3, 2]|$ and there is no need to swap the rows. To eliminate the element in the second column, i.e., $A[3, 2]$, the required replacement operation is

$$\{A|b\}[3, :] + \{A|b\}[2, :] \rightarrow \{A|b\}[3, :],$$

leading to

$$\begin{bmatrix} 3 & -1 & 4 & | & 11 \\ 0 & 5/3 & -14/3 & | & -19/3 \\ 0 & -5/3 & 2/3 & | & 7/3 \end{bmatrix} \rightarrow \begin{bmatrix} 3 & -1 & 4 & | & 11 \\ 0 & 5/3 & -14/3 & | & -19/3 \\ 0 & 0 & -4 & | & -4 \end{bmatrix}.$$

Finally, the backward substitution can be used to solve the system to obtain

$$\begin{bmatrix} x_1 \\ x_2 \\ x_3 \end{bmatrix} = \begin{bmatrix} 2 \\ -1 \\ 1 \end{bmatrix}.$$

Considering the steps of the Gaussian elimination with partial pivoting for this example, the corresponding LU factorization can be written as

$$\begin{bmatrix} 0 & 1 & 0 \\ 1 & 0 & 0 \\ 0 & 0 & 1 \end{bmatrix} \begin{bmatrix} 2 & 1 & -2 \\ 3 & -1 & 4 \\ 1 & -2 & 2 \end{bmatrix} = \begin{bmatrix} 1 & 0 & 0 \\ 2/3 & 1 & 0 \\ 1/3 & -1 & 1 \end{bmatrix} \begin{bmatrix} 3 & -1 & 4 \\ 0 & 5/3 & -14/3 \\ 0 & 0 & -4 \end{bmatrix},$$

where the permutation matrix (that premultiplies the system matrix) is designed for swapping rows 1 and 2 without changing the third row.

Table 7.1 presents time measurements with the Gaussian elimination programs described in this chapter. Matrix equations involving random elements are generated and used to measure the time required for eliminations. It is clearly visible that the additional time required for the partial pivoting is negligible, compared to the overall $\mathcal{O}(n^3)$ time required for the Gaussian elimination.

7.6   Further Topics

7.6.1 Banded Matrices

The Gaussian elimination and the LU factorization are basic methods for the solution of matrix equations involving general matrices. On the other hand, some matrices have special properties that can be exploited to improve their solutions. As an example, consider an $n \times n$ banded matrix A with bandwidth $p < n$, where $p = 2k + 1$ for $k > 0$. Note that, by definition,

$$A[i, j] = 0 \quad \text{if } |i - j| > k.$$

Then, the Gaussian elimination (or the LU factorization) can be performed more efficiently by considering that some elements are already zero and they are not required to be eliminated.

Tridiagonal matrices with bandwidths $p = 3$ (i.e., $k = 1$ in the formula above) are important examples of banded matrices. Consider a system $Ax = b$ involving an $n \times n$ tridiagonal matrix, i.e.,

$$
\begin{bmatrix}
a_{11} & a_{12} & 0 & 0 & \cdots & 0 & 0 \\
a_{21} & a_{22} & a_{23} & 0 & \cdots & 0 & 0 \\
0 & a_{32} & a_{33} & a_{34} & \cdots & 0 & 0 \\
0 & 0 & a_{43} & a_{44} & \cdots & 0 & 0 \\
\vdots & \vdots & \vdots & \vdots & \ddots & \vdots & \vdots \\
0 & 0 & 0 & 0 & \cdots & a_{(n-1)(n-1)} & a_{(n-1)n} \\
0 & 0 & 0 & 0 & \cdots & a_{n(n-1)} & a_{nn}
\end{bmatrix}
\begin{bmatrix}
x_1 \\ x_2 \\ x_3 \\ x_4 \\ \vdots \\ x_{n-1} \\ x_n
\end{bmatrix}
=
\begin{bmatrix}
b_1 \\ b_2 \\ b_3 \\ b_4 \\ \vdots \\ b_{n-1} \\ b_n
\end{bmatrix}.
$$

Using the Gaussian elimination, the first step is to eliminate the elements in the first column using the first row. However, for a tridiagonal matrix, we do not have to deal with whole rows and columns. In fact, in the first step, there is only one nonzero element to be eliminated in the second row, i.e., a_{21}. In addition, only one element of the matrix, i.e., a_{22}, needs an update while eliminating a_{21}. Hence, we can write the first step as

$$m_{21} = a_{21}/a_{11},$$

$$a_{22} - m_{21}a_{12} \to a_{22},$$

$$b_2 - m_{21}b_1 \to b_2,$$

followed by $a_{21} = 0$.

Next, in the second step, a_{32} is required to be eliminated using the updated value of a_{22}. The only element of the matrix that requires to be updated in this elimination step is a_{33}, and we have

$$m_{32} = a_{32}/a_{22},$$

$$a_{33} - m_{32}a_{23} \rightarrow a_{33},$$

$$b_3 - m_{32}b_2 \rightarrow b_3,$$

followed by $a_{32} = 0$.

It can be derived that, for a tridiagonal matrix, the elimination in the kth step (where $k < n$) can be written as

$$m_{(k+1)k} = a_{(k+1)k}/a_{kk},$$

$$a_{(k+1)(k+1)} - m_{(k+1)k}a_{k(k+1)} \rightarrow a_{(k+1)(k+1)},$$

$$b_{(k+1)} - m_{(k+1)k}b_k \rightarrow b_{(k+1)},$$

followed by $a_{(k+1)k} = 0$.

Hence, at the $(n-1)$th step, we have

$$m_{n(n-1)} = a_{n(n-1)}/a_{(n-1)(n-1)},$$

$$a_{nn} - m_{n(n-1)}a_{(n-1)n} \rightarrow a_{nn},$$

$$b_n - m_{n(n-1)}b_{(n-1)} \rightarrow b_n,$$

followed by $a_{n(n-1)} = 0$.

Considering the discussion above, a program of Gaussian elimination for tridiagonal matrices can be written as follows:

```
R Program: Gaussian Elimination for Tridiagonal Matrices (Original)

01 gaussianeliminationtridiagonal = function(Ab){
02    n = nrow(Ab)
03    for (k in (1:(n-1))){
04       multiplier = Ab[k+1,k]/Ab[k,k]
05       Ab[k+1,k] = 0
06       Ab[k+1,k+1] = Ab[k+1,k+1] - multiplier*Ab[k,k+1]
07       Ab[k+1,n+1] = Ab[k+1,n+1] - multiplier*Ab[k,n+1]
08    }
09    return(Ab)
10 }
```

In this program, the input is an $n \times (n+1)$ matrix Ab that includes the combination of the $n \times n$ matrix (that must be tridiagonal) and the right-hand-side vector. The output is the same matrix, including an $n \times n$ upper-triangular matrix (again tridiagonal) and the modified right-hand-side vector. The time complexity of the program above is only $\mathcal{O}(n)$. Hence, compared to the ordinary Gaussian elimination with $\mathcal{O}(n^3)$ complexity, this program is extremely efficient for large values of n.

Following Gaussian elimination, the solution of a matrix equation requires a backward substitution, which can also be improved for tridiagonal matrices. Consider an $n \times n$ matrix equation involving an upper-triangular and tridiagonal matrix, i.e.,

$$
\begin{bmatrix}
u_{11} & u_{12} & 0 & 0 & \cdots & 0 & 0 \\
0 & u_{22} & u_{23} & 0 & \cdots & 0 & 0 \\
0 & 0 & u_{33} & u_{34} & \cdots & 0 & 0 \\
0 & 0 & 0 & u_{44} & \cdots & 0 & 0 \\
\vdots & \vdots & \vdots & \vdots & \ddots & \vdots & \vdots \\
0 & 0 & 0 & 0 & \cdots & u_{(n-1)(n-1)} & u_{(n-1)n} \\
0 & 0 & 0 & 0 & \cdots & 0 & u_{nn}
\end{bmatrix}
\begin{bmatrix}
x_1 \\ x_2 \\ x_3 \\ x_4 \\ \vdots \\ x_{n-1} \\ x_n
\end{bmatrix}
=
\begin{bmatrix}
b_1 \\ b_2 \\ b_3 \\ b_4 \\ \vdots \\ b_{n-1} \\ b_n
\end{bmatrix}.
$$

Note that there are only two nonzero elements per row, except the last row with only one element u_{nn}. The required operations in the backward substitution can be written as

$$x_n = b_n/u_{nn},$$

$$x_{n-1} = (b_{n-1} - u_{(n-1)n}x_n)/u_{(n-1)(n-1)},$$

$$x_{n-2} = (b_{n-2} - u_{(n-2)(n-1)}x_{(n-1)})/u_{(n-2)(n-2)},$$

$$\vdots$$

$$x_1 = (b_1 - u_{12}x_2)/u_{11}.$$

The program can be written as follows:

```
R Program: Backward Substitution for Tridiagonal Matrices (Original)

01 backwardsubtridiagonal = function(U,b){
02    x = c(0)
03    n = nrow(U)
04    for (i in (n:1)){
05        x[i] = b[i]
06        if (i < n){
07            x[i] = x[i] - U[i,i+1]*x[i+1]
08        }
09        x[i] = x[i]/U[i,i]
10    }
11    return(cbind(x))
12 }
```

As opposed to the ordinary backward substitution program (with $\mathcal{O}(n^2)$ complexity), the time complexity of this program is $\mathcal{O}(n)$. As a result, the solution of an $n \times n$ system involving a tridiagonal matrix requires $\mathcal{O}(n)$ processing time overall.

Both programs above are superior to the corresponding programs for ordinary matrices in terms of the processing time. However, the memory complexity is the same, and it is $\mathcal{O}(n^2)$ for all programs. This is because, storing a matrix and a right-hand-side vector requires $\mathcal{O}(n^2)$ space. On the other hand, it is possible to store the elements of a tridiagonal matrix in a vector of $\mathcal{O}(n)$ elements by omitting zero elements. This would reduce the memory down to $\mathcal{O}(n)$ at the cost of some indexing operations to use the matrix elements properly.

7.6.2 Cholesky Factorization

Consider an $n \times n$ real matrix A. The matrix is called positive definite if

$$x^T A x > 0$$

for all nonzero vectors x with real elements. It can be shown that, if A is symmetric and positive definite, then it can be factorized as

$$A = LL^T,$$

where L is a lower-triangular matrix with positive diagonal elements. This is called the Cholesky factorization, which is a common technique to solve matrix equations involving symmetric positive-definite matrices.

Let A be a symmetric positive-definite matrix with a Cholesky factorization as

$$
\begin{bmatrix}
a_{11} & a_{21} & \cdots & a_{n1} \\
a_{21} & a_{22} & \cdots & a_{n2} \\
a_{31} & a_{32} & \cdots & a_{n3} \\
\vdots & \vdots & \ddots & \vdots \\
a_{n1} & a_{n2} & \cdots & a_{nn}
\end{bmatrix}
$$

$$
=
\begin{bmatrix}
l_{11} & 0 & 0 & \cdots & 0 \\
l_{21} & l_{22} & 0 & \cdots & 0 \\
l_{31} & l_{32} & l_{33} & \cdots & 0 \\
\vdots & \vdots & \vdots & \ddots & \vdots \\
l_{n1} & l_{n2} & l_{n3} & \cdots & l_{nn}
\end{bmatrix}
\begin{bmatrix}
l_{11} & l_{21} & l_{31} & \cdots & l_{n1} \\
0 & l_{22} & l_{32} & \cdots & l_{n2} \\
0 & 0 & l_{33} & \cdots & l_{n3} \\
\vdots & \vdots & \vdots & \ddots & \vdots \\
0 & 0 & 0 & \cdots & l_{nn}
\end{bmatrix}.
$$

Considering the multiplication of the two matrices (particularly omitting the zero elements), we have

$$a_{11} = (l_{11})^2 \to l_{11} = (a_{11})^{1/2}.$$

Hence, l_{11} can be calculated just by using a_{11}. We also note that

$$a_{j1} = l_{11} l_{j1}$$

or

$$l_{j1} = a_{j1}/l_{11}, \quad j = 2, 3, \ldots, n.$$

Next, the nonzero elements in the second column of L can be calculated as

$$l_{22} = \left(a_{22} - l_{21}^2\right)^{1/2},$$

followed by

$$l_{j2} = (a_{j2} - l_{j1} l_{21})/l_{22}, \quad j = 3, 4, \ldots, n.$$

In general, for $2 \leq i \leq n$, one can derive

$$l_{ii} = \left(a_{ii} - \sum_{k=1}^{i-1} l_{ik}^2\right)^{1/2}$$

and

$$l_{ji} = \left(a_{ji} - \sum_{k=1}^{i-1} l_{jk}l_{ik}\right)\Big/l_{ii}, \quad j = (i+1), (i+2), \ldots, n,$$

to compute the other elements of the factor L.

At this stage, we can write a program for the Cholesky factorization as below. In this program, the input is an $n \times n$ matrix A to be factorized. The output is an $n \times n$ matrix including the lower-triangular matrix of the factorization. Note that the upper-triangular part can be obtained via a simple transpose operation.

```
R Program: Cholesky Factorization (Original)

01 choleskyfactorization = function(A){
02     n = nrow(A)
03     L = matrix(0,nrow=n,ncol=n)
04     for (i in (1:n)){
05         L[i,i] = A[i,i]
06         if (i > 1){
07             for (k in (1:(i-1))){
08                 L[i,i] = L[i,i] - L[i,k]*L[i,k]
09             }
10         }
11         L[i,i] = (L[i,i])^(1/2)
12         if (i < n){
13             for (j in ((i+1):n)){
14                 L[j,i] = A[j,i]
15                 if (i > 1){
16                     for (k in (1:(i-1))){
17                         L[j,i] = L[j,i] - L[j,k]*L[i,k]
18                     }
19                 }
20                 L[j,i] = L[j,i]/L[i,i]
21             }
22         }
23     }
24     return(L)
25 }
```

Similar to the LU factorization (and the Gaussian elimination), the time complexity of the Cholesky factorization is $\mathcal{O}(n^3)$. For a detailed analysis, however, consider a critical line 17, which is executed for

$$\sum_{i=2}^{n-1} (i-1)(n-i) = n\sum_{i=2}^{n-1} i - \sum_{i=2}^{n-1} i^2 - n\sum_{i=2}^{n-1} 1 + \sum_{i=2}^{n-1} i$$

times. Evaluating the summations, we get

$$\sum_{i=2}^{n-1}(i-1)(n-i) \approx \frac{n^3}{6}.$$

Comparing the last expression with the cost of the LU factorization or the Gaussian elimination, it can be seen that the time complexity is halved by using the Cholesky factorization (even though its order is the same, $\mathcal{O}(n^3)$). For this reason, if a system involves a symmetric positive-definite matrix, the Cholesky factorization can be preferred over the LU factorization.

7.6.3 Gauss–Jordan Elimination

Using the Gaussian elimination on a matrix makes it upper triangular so that it can be solved via a backward substitution. On the other hand, it is possible to convert the same matrix into a diagonal one and perform a simple solution involving a diagonal matrix. This process, which is quite similar to the ordinary Gaussian elimination, is called the Gauss–Jordan elimination. A program can be written as follows:

```
R Program: Gauss–Jordan Elimination (Original)

01 gaussjordanelimination = function(Ab){
02     n = nrow(Ab)
03     for (k in (1:n))){
04         if (k > 1){
05             for (i in (1:(k-1))){
06                 mik = Ab[i,k]/Ab[k,k]
07                 Ab[i,k] = 0
08                 for (j in ((k+1):(n+1))){
09                     Ab[i,j] = Ab[i,j] - mik*Ab[k,j]
10                 }
11             }
12         }
13         if (k < n){
14             for (i in ((k+1):n)){
15                 mik = Ab[i,k]/Ab[k,k]
16                 Ab[i,k] = 0
17                 for (j in ((k+1):(n+1))){
18                     Ab[i,j] = Ab[i,j] - mik*Ab[k,j]
19                 }
20             }
21         }
22     }
23     return(Ab)
24 }
```

Note that, as opposed to the Gaussian elimination, this program has two inner loops. The loop

```
        for (i in (1:(k-1))){
```

is for eliminating elements under the diagonal, whereas the loop

```
for (i in ((k+1):n)){
```
is for eliminating those above the diagonal. Consequently, the cost of the elimination is doubled, compared to the Gaussian elimination program. Therefore, the Gauss–Jordan elimination is preferred only when obtaining a diagonal matrix is essential, e.g., when inverting matrices as discussed below.

7.6.4 Determinant

Determinant is an important quantity for square matrices. For example, a system involving a square matrix has a unique solution if and only if its determinant is nonzero. As discussed in Chap. 3, the determinant of a matrix can be calculated recursively, but this is an expensive method with $\mathcal{O}(n!)$ time complexity. A better way is to calculate the determinant via the LU factorization as follows.

Consider the LU decomposition of an $n \times n$ square matrix $A = LU$. Using the properties of the determinant, we have

$$\det(A) = \det(L)\det(U).$$

The determinant of a triangular matrix is the multiplication of its diagonal elements. Hence,

$$\det(A) = \det(U) = \prod_{i=1}^{n} U[i,i],$$

noting that the diagonal elements in L are unity, i.e., $\det(L) = 1$. Considering the LU factorization, the time complexity of this method is $\mathcal{O}(n^3)$, which is much better than the $\mathcal{O}(n!)$ complexity of the recursive method.

7.6.5 Inverting Matrices

Matrix equations can be solved by inverting matrices. Consider a system $Ax = b$, where A is an $n \times n$ matrix with nonzero determinant. The solution can be written as

$$x = A^{-1}b,$$

where A^{-1} is an $n \times n$ matrix, which is the inverse of A.

In this book, we focus on how to solve matrix equations using the Gaussian elimination or the LU factorization. In fact, matrices are rarely inverted since the Gaussian elimination and the LU factorization are available to solve linear systems, and direct methods (such as the Cramer's rule) are expensive and/or unstable. If the inverse of a matrix must be found, one can still use the Gaussian elimination, the LU factorization, or the Gauss–Jordan elimination.

Let A be an $n \times n$ matrix to be inverted and consider a linear system of equations in the form of

$$AX = I,$$

where I is the $n \times n$ identity matrix, and X is an $n \times n$ matrix with unknown elements. We note that, if A has an inverse, then $A^{-1} = X$. The overall system above can be considered as n systems

$$Ax_i = e_i, \quad i = 1, 2, \ldots, n,$$

where x_i and e_i are the columns of X and I, respectively. When the vectors x_i are solved using the Gaussian elimination or the LU factorization, one can obtain $X = A^{-1}$ as the inverse matrix.

Using the Gauss–Jordan elimination is particularly suitable for inverting matrices. Consider an $n \times 2n$ augmented matrix $[A|I]$. Using the Gauss–Jordan elimination, we have

$$[A|I] \to [D|DA^{-1}],$$

where D is a diagonal matrix. The rows of the resulting augmented matrix can be further scaled as

$$[D|DA^{-1}] \to [D^{-1}D|D^{-1}DA^{-1}] = [I|A^{-1}],$$

and the inverse of the matrix becomes available in the second part of the final result.

7.7 Conclusions

Since they are used to model real-life scenarios, linear systems of equations are extremely important in many application areas. Their solutions are also important, especially on computers that can handle large matrix equations. The Gaussian elimination and the LU factorization are two famous (and related) methods to solve such equations involving dense matrices. Both methods rely on the fact that triangular matrix equations are easy to solve by substitution and it is possible to convert dense matrix equations into triangular matrix equations via elimination. Both methods are commonly used with partial pivoting to avoid numerical problems due to null diagonal elements and rounding errors. The Gaussian elimination and the LU factorization can also be improved for different systems (e.g., those involving banded matrices), whereas alternative methods become available for special cases (e.g., symmetric positive-definite matrices). In the last chapter, we consider the design of simple systems using matrix equations and their solutions.

7.8   Exercises

1. Consider an overdetermined system involving three equations and two unknowns as

$$\begin{bmatrix} 2 & 1 \\ -1 & 4 \\ -2 & a_{32} \end{bmatrix} \begin{bmatrix} x_1 \\ x_2 \end{bmatrix} = \begin{bmatrix} 1 \\ -5 \\ 0 \end{bmatrix}.$$

Find the value of a_{32} such that the system has a unique solution.

2. Consider an underdetermined system involving two equations and three unknowns as

$$\begin{bmatrix} 1 & 2 & -1 \\ 4 & 8 & a_{23} \end{bmatrix} \begin{bmatrix} x_1 \\ x_2 \\ x_3 \end{bmatrix} = \begin{bmatrix} 1 \\ -5 \end{bmatrix}.$$

Find the value of a_{23} such that the system has no solution.

3. Consider a square system involving three equations and three unknowns as

$$\begin{bmatrix} 1 & -2 & 3 \\ 2 & -1 & 4 \\ 4 & -2 & a_{33} \end{bmatrix} \begin{bmatrix} x_1 \\ x_2 \\ x_3 \end{bmatrix} = \begin{bmatrix} 7 \\ 12 \\ b_3 \end{bmatrix}.$$

- Suggest values for a_{33} and b_3 such that the system has infinitely many solutions.
- Suggest values for a_{33} and b_3 such that the system has no solution.
- Suggest values for a_{33} and b_3 such that the system has a unique solution.

4. Write a program that performs forward substitution to solve any system involving a lower triangular matrix. The inputs should be an $n \times n$ lower triangular matrix L and a right-hand-side vector b. The output should be the solution vector x in $Lx = b$. Test your code for the following matrix equations:

- $$\begin{bmatrix} 5 & 0 & 0 \\ 2 & -3 & 0 \\ 4 & 2 & -4 \end{bmatrix} \begin{bmatrix} x_1 \\ x_2 \\ x_3 \end{bmatrix} = \begin{bmatrix} 5 \\ 8 \\ -12 \end{bmatrix}$$

- $$\begin{bmatrix} 2 & 0 & 0 & 0 \\ -2 & 3 & 0 & 0 \\ 1 & -4 & 8 & 0 \\ -3 & 0 & 1 & -2 \end{bmatrix} \begin{bmatrix} x_1 \\ x_2 \\ x_3 \\ x_4 \end{bmatrix} = \begin{bmatrix} 2 \\ -8 \\ 9 \\ -9 \end{bmatrix}$$

5. Write a program that performs backward substitution to solve any system involving an upper triangular matrix. The inputs should be an $n \times n$ upper triangular matrix U and a right-hand-side vector b. The output should be the solution vector x in $Ux = b$. Test your code for the following matrix equations:

- $$\begin{bmatrix} -2 & 4 & 2 \\ 0 & -3 & 5 \\ 0 & 0 & -2 \end{bmatrix} \begin{bmatrix} x_1 \\ x_2 \\ x_3 \end{bmatrix} = \begin{bmatrix} 4 \\ -21 \\ 6 \end{bmatrix}$$

- $$\begin{bmatrix} 1 & -5 & 2 & 9 \\ 0 & 2 & -3 & -1 \\ 0 & 0 & 7 & -2 \\ 0 & 0 & 0 & -4 \end{bmatrix} \begin{bmatrix} x_1 \\ x_2 \\ x_3 \\ x_4 \end{bmatrix} = \begin{bmatrix} 5 \\ 5 \\ -6 \\ -12 \end{bmatrix}$$

6. Write a program that performs the Gaussian elimination without pivoting to solve a given system involving an $n \times n$ matrix A and a right-hand-side vector b. The input should be the $n \times (n + 1)$ augmented matrix $[A|b]$. The output should be the same augmented matrix after elimination. Test your code for the following matrix equations:

- $$\begin{bmatrix} 4 & -1 & -7 \\ 2 & 1 & -3 \\ -1 & 2 & 4 \end{bmatrix} \begin{bmatrix} x_1 \\ x_2 \\ x_3 \end{bmatrix} = \begin{bmatrix} 0 \\ -2 \\ 1 \end{bmatrix}$$

- $$\begin{bmatrix} 1 & 4 & 7 \\ 2 & 5 & 8 \\ 3 & 6 & -9 \end{bmatrix} \begin{bmatrix} x_1 \\ x_2 \\ x_3 \end{bmatrix} = \begin{bmatrix} 1 \\ 2 \\ 3 \end{bmatrix}$$

- $$\begin{bmatrix} 1 & -2 & 1 \\ 2 & 0 & 2 \\ 1 & 0 & 1 \end{bmatrix} \begin{bmatrix} x_1 \\ x_2 \\ x_3 \end{bmatrix} = \begin{bmatrix} -2 \\ 4 \\ 2 \end{bmatrix}$$

- $$\begin{bmatrix} 1 & 2 & 3 \\ 2 & 4 & 2 \\ -4 & 2 & 1 \end{bmatrix} \begin{bmatrix} x_1 \\ x_2 \\ x_3 \end{bmatrix} = \begin{bmatrix} 1 \\ 2 \\ 3 \end{bmatrix}$$

What can be said about the solution of the third and fourth matrix equations considering the corresponding outputs?

7. Measure the time required to apply the Gaussian elimination to a system of 50 equations involving random elements as

```
Ab = matrix(rnorm(50^2+50),nrow=50)
system.time(gaussianelimination(Ab))
```

Repeat your measurement for $n = 100$ and $n = 200$, and analyze your timing results.

8. Write a program that finds the LU factorization of a given matrix without pivoting. The input should be an $n \times n$ matrix A. The outputs should be the factors L and U in $A = LU$. Test your code for the following matrices:

- $A = \begin{bmatrix} 4 & -1 & -7 \\ 2 & 1 & -3 \\ -1 & 2 & 4 \end{bmatrix}$

- $A = \begin{bmatrix} 1 & -2 & 1 \\ 2 & 0 & 2 \\ 1 & 0 & 1 \end{bmatrix}$

- $A = \begin{bmatrix} 1 & -3 & 1 & 1 \\ 1 & 1 & 4 & -4 \\ -1 & 3 & 2 & 2 \\ 2 & -8 & 2 & 1 \end{bmatrix}$

9. Suggest and write an in-place program that performs LU factorization without allocating any extra memory (other than scalars). Note that the lower and upper triangular parts can be put in a single matrix while omitting the diagonal (involving unity elements) of the lower triangular factor.

10. Write a program that performs the Gaussian elimination with partial pivoting to solve a given system involving an $n \times n$ matrix A and a right-hand-side vector b. The input should be the $n \times (n + 1)$ augmented matrix $[A|b]$. The output should be the same augmented matrix after elimination. Test your code for the following matrix equations:

- $\begin{bmatrix} 0 & 0 & 3 \\ -2 & 0 & 2 \\ 1 & 2 & 0 \end{bmatrix} \begin{bmatrix} x_1 \\ x_2 \\ x_3 \end{bmatrix} = \begin{bmatrix} 1 \\ 2 \\ 3 \end{bmatrix}$

- $\begin{bmatrix} 0 & 1 & -2 \\ 2 & 0 & -1 \\ -2 & 4 & 0 \end{bmatrix} \begin{bmatrix} x_1 \\ x_2 \\ x_3 \end{bmatrix} = \begin{bmatrix} 0 \\ 5 \\ 2 \end{bmatrix}$

- $\begin{bmatrix} 1 & 2 & 3 \\ 2 & 4 & 2 \\ -4 & 2 & 1 \end{bmatrix} \begin{bmatrix} x_1 \\ x_2 \\ x_3 \end{bmatrix} = \begin{bmatrix} 1 \\ 2 \\ 3 \end{bmatrix}$

11. Measure the time required to apply the Gaussian elimination with partial pivoting to a system of 50 equations involving random elements as

```
Ab = matrix(rnorm(50^2+50),nrow=50)
system.time(gaussianeliminationpartial(Ab))
```

Repeat your measurement for $n = 100$ and $n = 200$ and analyze your timing results. Compare with your previous results obtained by using the Gaussian elimination without pivoting. Also, based on your measurement for $n = 200$, estimate the time that would be required to apply the Gaussian elimination with partial pivoting to a system with $n = 2000$ and $n = 20000$.

12. Write a program that applies Gaussian elimination for tridiagonal matrices. Also implement the backward substitution for tridiagonal matrices and use your programs to solve the system

$$
\begin{bmatrix}
1 & 1 & 0 & 0 & 0 & 0 \\
1 & 2 & 3 & 0 & 0 & 0 \\
0 & 3 & 3 & 4 & 0 & 0 \\
0 & 0 & 3 & 4 & 5 & 0 \\
0 & 0 & 0 & 4 & 5 & 6 \\
0 & 0 & 0 & 0 & 5 & 6
\end{bmatrix}
\begin{bmatrix}
x_1 \\ x_2 \\ x_3 \\ x_4 \\ x_5 \\ x_6
\end{bmatrix}
=
\begin{bmatrix}
1 \\ 2 \\ 3 \\ 4 \\ 5 \\ 6
\end{bmatrix}.
$$

13. Write a program that finds the Cholesky factorization of a given positive-definite matrix. Apply your program to factorize

$$
\begin{bmatrix}
1 & 3 & 2 \\
3 & 10 & 7 \\
2 & 7 & 9
\end{bmatrix}.
$$

The Cholesky factorization immediately fails if $A[1, 1] = 0$. What does this mean?

14. Using your LU factorization program (Question 8), find the determinant of the matrix

$$
\begin{bmatrix}
1 & 2 & -1 \\
1 & -2 & 1 \\
2 & -1 & 1
\end{bmatrix}.
$$

Check your result using the built-in function of R as

```
det(matrix(c(1,1,2,2,-2,-1,-1,1,1),nrow=3))
```

File Processing

8

As we described in the first chapter, a computer program is written to effectively solve a given problem, which may involve calculations, data processing, or both. In general, given a code segment, it may not be easy to separate calculations and data processing. For example, the computation of the 1-norm of a given vector can be considered as processing the given vector (data processing) and adding the absolute values of its elements (calculations). On the other hand, some applications (such as sorting) can be considered as mostly data processing, whereas others (such as finding Fibonacci numbers) can be considered as mostly calculations.

In this chapter, we focus on file processing, i.e., processing files for given purposes, which can be considered as data processing. Specifically, we write and analyze programs to investigate and modify files. As opposed to many other problems in computer science, file processing is usually very dependent on the syntax of the programming language. Some languages, such as R, provide many higher-level functions that can easily be used to perform complex input/output operations, whereas others may need more programmer efforts. In this chapter, we attack only some basic problems, whose solutions can easily be performed using different programming languages.

As shown below, we consider files that contain numbers or some texts. Dealing with texts means that we may get a constant, a variable, an input, or an output containing a character or a set of characters rather than numbers. In computer science, such nonnumeric items are commonly called as *strings*. Strings can also be collected in vectors, leading to vectors of strings.

8.1   Investigating Files

Consider a file intro.txt, which contains the following text:

Ö. Ergül, *Guide to Programming and Algorithms Using R*,
DOI 10.1007/978-1-4471-5328-3_8,
© Springer-Verlag London 2013

A computer program is a sequence of commands and instructions to
effectively solve a given problem. Such a problem may involve
calculations, data processing, or both. Each computer program is
based on an underlying procedure called algorithm. An algorithm
may be implemented in different ways, leading to different
programs using the same procedure. We follow this convention
throughout this book, where an algorithm refers to a list of
procedures whereas a program refers to its implementation as a
code.

As the first exercise, let us write a program that counts the number of words in a
text file, i.e., intro.txt in this case. The algorithm is based on splitting the text into
strings at spaces and counting the number of resulting partitions. This can easily be
done using built-in functions of R as follows:

```
R Program: Counting Words in a Text File (Original)

01 countwords = function(){
02    v = scan("intro.txt","",quiet=TRUE)
03    print(paste("The file has",length(v),"words."))
04 }
```

This short program starts by reading the file intro.txt as

```
v = scan("intro.txt","",quiet=TRUE)
```

using the scan command of R. In the above, quiet=TRUE is required option-
ally to avoid any message from scan that normally prints out the number of items
scanned. By using an equality above, we assign the scanned words into a vector v.
Hence, we easily split the text and put the words into a vector. The length of this
vector gives the number of words in the file. Hence, using the program as

```
countwords()
```

we get an output like

```
"The file has 79 words."
```

Note that we use the paste command to combine the items to be printed.

The program above does not have any input and is written to count the number
of words in a fixed file, namely, intro.txt, which must exist in the program directory.
Alternatively, a general program for reading any text file can be written as follows:

```
R Program: Counting Words in a General Text File (Original)

01 countwordsgeneral = function(filename){
02    v = scan(filename,"",quiet=TRUE)
03    print(paste("The file has",length(v),"words."))
04 }
```

Here, the name of the file to be read is provided as an input string `filename`, which is then used in the `scan` command. For example, this program can be used as

`countwordsgeneral("intro.txt")`

to find the number of words in intro.txt. Note that both programs above give an error if the file to be read does not exist in the working directory.

Next, consider the following program, which reads words from a file and writes them as separate lines into another file. When doing this, we also would like to remove punctuation marks, i.e., "." and ",", from the words.

R Program: Partitioning a Text into Words (Original)

```
01 partitiontextgeneral = function(inputfile,outputfile){
02    v = scan(inputfile,"",quiet=TRUE)
03    w = unlist(strsplit(v,"[.,]+"))
04    write(w,outputfile,sep="",append=FALSE)
05 }
```

In the above, the vector v again contains the words of a given text. After forming this vector, the punctuation marks are removed as

`w = unlist(strsplit(v,"[.,]+"))`

where the resulting punctuation-free words are stored in w. Finally, this vector is written into an output file whose name is the input string `outputfile`. Using the program above for the file intro.txt as

`partitiontextgeneral("intro.txt","wordsofintro.txt")`

creates a new file wordsofintro.txt that contains the words as

```
A
computer
program
is
a
sequence
of
commands
and
instructions
to
effectively
solve
a
given
problem
Such
:
```

Note that each word is written as a separate line without any punctuation marks.

Depending on the application, text files can be processed in many different ways. For example, after partitioning a given text into words, one can easily omit the one-letter words "A" and "a" while writing the words into the output file. Consider the following program for this purpose:

```
R Program: Partitioning a Text into Words Omitting A (Original)

01 partitiontextgeneralomit = function(inputfile,outputfile){
02     v = scan(inputfile,"",quiet=TRUE)
03     w = unlist(strsplit(v,"[.,]+"))
04     for (i in 1:length(w)){
05         if ((w[i] != "a") && (w[i] != "A")){
06             write(w[i],outputfile,sep="",append=TRUE)
07         }
08     }
09 }
```

In this program, the words stored in vector w are written manually one by one into the selected output file. In order to omit the one-letter words, a conditional statement is used as

```
if ((w[i] != "a") && (w[i] != "A")){
```

which holds when the ith element of w is neither "a" nor "A". If this is the case, then

```
write(w[i],outputfile,sep="",append=TRUE)
```

is used to write w[i] into the output file. Consequently, using the program as

```
partitiontextgeneralomit("intro.txt","wordsofintro_noa.txt")
```

creates a file wordsofintro_noa.txt containing only non-a-words of intro.txt.

In the final program above, append=TRUE is used in the write statement, considering that the words in vector w need to be written in the same file one by one. Here, setting append to TRUE means that a letter w[i] should be written into the file as a new line without deleting previous lines. Hence, one needs to be careful when employing this program for multiple times. For example, using

```
partitiontextgeneralomit("intro.txt","wordsofintro_noa.txt")
partitiontextgeneralomit("intro.txt","wordsofintro_noa.txt")
partitiontextgeneralomit("intro.txt","wordsofintro_noa.txt")
```

where the function is called three times for the same file names, produces an output file wordsofintro_noa.txt that contains the list of words repeated for three times. Of course, appending may actually be desired, for example, if some words in different input files are required to be collected in a single output file, e.g., as

```
partitiontextgeneralomit("intro1.txt","wordsofintro_noa.txt")
partitiontextgeneralomit("intro2.txt","wordsofintro_noa.txt")
partitiontextgeneralomit("intro3.txt","wordsofintro_noa.txt")
```

where intro1.txt, intro2.txt, and intro3.txt are different input files. But, in general, programmers need to be careful while setting the append flag in write statements.

Another issue that must be considered carefully when processing files is regarding the choice of input and output files. In general, output files should be different than input files to avoid mixing output and input data. In fact, if there are no storage limitations, it is not uncommon to use different files as input and output, even when the program can work using a single file. A good reason for such an effort to use separate files may be a need for keeping the input file to use later, while the output file is produced safely. On the other hand, using the same file as both input and output may be preferred, especially when the main purpose is modifying a given file rather than processing it.

Next, consider the following program that finds the longest word in a given text file:

```
R Program: Finding the Longest Word in a Text File (Original)

01 findlongestword = function(filename){
02     v = scan(filename,"",quiet=TRUE)
03     w = unlist(strsplit(v,"[.,]+"))
04     maxwordlength = 0
05     longestword = ""
06     for (i in 1:length(w)){
07         wordlength = nchar(w[i])
08         if (wordlength > maxwordlength){
09             longestword = w[i]
10             maxwordlength = wordlength
11         }
12     }
13     print(paste(longestword,"has",maxwordlength,"letters."))
14 }
```

Similar to the previous programs, this program needs an input file whose name is specified by the input string filename. After reading a given file and processing its words by removing punctuation marks, a for loop is constructed to go through the words and to find the longest one. Hence, the loop variable i changes from 1 to length(w), where w is the vector containing the words. Before the loop, the variables maxwordlength and longestword, which store the maximum word length and the corresponding word, respectively, are set to 0 and "". These variables are updated inside the loop whenever any considered word w[i] is the longest word encountered so far. This is checked by an if statement in line 08. Note that the number of letters in a string can easily be found by using the built-in function nchar. After the loop is completed, the final values of maxwordlength and longestword are printed out as a message. For example, using the program for intro.txt as

```
findlongestword("intro.txt")
```

leads to an output like

```
                    "implementation has 14 letters."
```

This means that the word "implementation" with 14 letters is the longest one in intro.txt.

Next, assume that we would like to analyze the text in a given input file by creating a histogram for all word lengths. Specifically, we would like to create a plot for the number of letters in a given set of words. Consider the following program for this purpose:

```
R Program: Checking Word Lengths in a Text File (Original)

01 checkwordlengths = function(filename){
02     v = scan(filename,"",quiet=TRUE)
03     w = unlist(strsplit(v,"[.,]+"))
04     z = 0
05     maxwordlength = 0
06     longestword = ""
07     for (i in 1:length(w)){
08         wordlength = nchar(w[i])
09         if (wordlength > maxwordlength){
10             longestword = w[i]
11             maxwordlength = wordlength
12         }
13         z[i] = wordlength
14     }
15     hist(z,breaks=maxwordlength)
16 }
```

Using this program for intro.txt creates a plot such as the one shown in Fig. 8.1. In this figure, the number of words is plotted with respect to the word length from 1 to 14. For example, there are a total of 11 words with three letters. In order to create such a plot, we use

```
            hist(z,breaks=maxwordlength)
```

where z is a vector that contains the length of each word, and `maxwordlength` is the number of letters in the longest word. The vector z is filled via a `for` loop by considering the words in a given text one by one. The value of `maxwordlength` is determined by the same loop using a procedure that is similar to one in the previous program. In fact, except the output statements, there are only two differences between the program above and the previous one. These are the initialization of the vector z in line 04 and setting the ith element of this vector in line 13.

8.2   Modifying Files

In the previous section, we consider programs to process a given file to produce an output, e.g., another file, a print, or a plot. In this section, we focus on modifying (updating) files for some purposes. Hence, for these programs, input and output are the same file. Using R, modifying a file is relatively easy since reading and writing commands are very flexible and gives the programmer many options via flags. In

Fig. 8.1 A histogram of
words in the file intro.txt

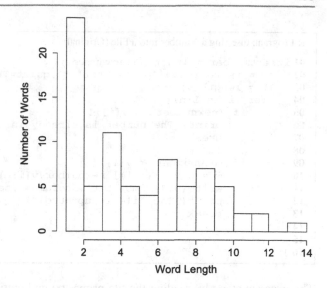

some other languages and platforms, using the same item both as an input and as an output may not be feasible or reliable. In such a case, the output can be created as a new file, which is then used to replace the input file via a copy–paste in the system level.

To demonstrate some file modifications that can be programmed, we consider a file primes.txt that contains prime numbers in the ascending order with possible jumps. Each number is written as a separate line, e.g.,

```
 2
 3
 5
 7
11
19
23
71
 ⋮
```

Our aim is to keep and update this file by inserting and deleting numbers.

First, assume that we would like to insert a new number to the file. The following program can be used for this purpose:

```
R Program: Inserting a Number into a File (Original)
01 insertnumber = function(newnumber){
02    v = strtoi(scan("primes.txt","",quiet=TRUE))
03    n = length(v)
04    for (i in 1:n){
05        if (newnumber == v[i]){
06            print("The number is already in the list!")
07            break
08        }
09        if (newnumber < v[i]){
10            w = c(v[1:(i-1)],newnumber,v[i:n])
11            write(w,"primes.txt",ncolumn=1,sep="",append=FALSE)
12            print("The file is updated!")
13            break
14        }
15    }
16 }
```

The program starts by reading the file primes.txt and putting the existing numbers into a vector v. Since the scan command of R creates strings or vectors of strings, conversions into integers are required via a built-in function strtoi. Hence, the vector v contains integers, i.e., prime numbers. Also note that the numbers in the file are assumed to be sorted in the ascending order. This way, any new number can be inserted in its correct place. The number to be inserted is stored in an input called newnumber. The program is based on comparing this number with those already exist in the file. Hence a for loop is constructed from 1 to n, where n is the length of the vector, i.e., the number of integers in the original text file. If the number to be inserted is equal to one of the numbers in v, the program prints a warning message (indicating that the number is already in the list) and the loop is broken without any modification on the file. Otherwise, the loop continues (hence the loop variable i is incremented) until the number to be inserted (newnumber) is smaller than the ith element (v[i]). This way, we find the correct location where the new number is to be inserted. The insertion is performed by simply using

$$w = c(v[1:(i-1)],newnumber,v[i:n])$$

and creating a new vector w using the numbers in v as well as the new number. This vector is finally written back into the file primes.txt as

$$write(w,"primes.txt",ncolumn=1,sep="",append=FALSE)$$

where append=FALSE is used to overwrite the file. Once the file is written, there is no need to maintain the loop; hence, a break command is used after a message is printed out to indicate the successful insertion.

As an example, if primes.txt contains $2, 3, 5, 7, 11, 19, \ldots$, then using the program above as

$$insertnumber(13)$$

updates the file by inserting a new line, i.e., 13, between 11 and 19.

Next, we consider the following program that can be used to delete a number from the file primes.txt:

```
R Program: Deleting a Number from a File (Original)

01 deletenumber = function(thenumber){
02     v = strtoi(scan("primes.txt","",quiet=TRUE))
03     n = length(v)
04     checkflag = 0
05     for (i in 1:n){
06         if (thenumber == v[i]){
07             w = c(v[1:(i-1)],v[(i+1):n])
08             write(w,"primes.txt",ncolumn=1,sep="",append=FALSE)
09             print("The number is deleted!")
10             checkflag = 1
11             break
12         }
13     }
14     if (checkflag == 0){
15         print("The number is not found!")
16     }
17 }
```

Similar to the previous program, this program starts by reading the file and storing the numbers in a vector v. Then, a `for` loop is constructed to go over these numbers and find the number to be deleted that is given by the input string `thenumber`. Once the number is found at the ith location, a new vector is created as

$$w = c(v[1:(i-1)],v[(i+1):n])$$

where w is nothing but the vector v except v[i]. After w is formed, it is written into primes.txt with `append=FALSE` so that the file is overwritten. After the write operation, a `break` command is used to avoid unnecessary checks. But, before the loop is broken, a flag `checkflag` is set to one. This flag is used to check whether the given number is deleted or not, and it is initialized as zero (indicating not deleted) before the loop because it is quite possible that the number to be deleted is not in the text file and the delete operation cannot be done. After the loop finishes, naturally or via break, `checkflag` is controlled, and a warning message is printed out if its value is zero, i.e., if the number is not found.

8.3   Working with Multiple Files

Considering different applications, it is quite common for a program to have multiple input and/or output files. In this section, we focus on simple programs with two input files, whose contents are compared with each other.

Consider two files including different numbers. We assume that, in both files, each number is written as a separate line and there is no repetition, while the numbers are not necessarily sorted (i.e., they are in mixed order). Our aim is to compare the numbers in these files and to find the total number of matches between the two sets. A simple algorithm for this purpose can be comparing the numbers one by one and printing out the number of matches once all comparisons are made. Hence, the following program can be used:

```
R Program: Comparing Numbers in Two Different Files (Original)

01 comparenumbers = function(filename1,filename2){
02     v = strtoi(scan(filename1,"",quiet=TRUE))
03     w = strtoi(scan(filename2,"",quiet=TRUE))
04     n = length(v)
05     m = length(w)
06     numberofmatches = 0
07     for (i in 1:n){
08         vnumber = v[i]
09         for (j in 1:m){
10             wnumber = w[j]
11             if (vnumber == wnumber){
12                 numberofmatches = numberofmatches + 1
13             }
14         }
15     }
16     print(paste("Length of the first file:",n))
17     print(paste("Length of the second file:",m))
18     print(paste("Number of matches:",numberofmatches))
19 }
```

The program starts by reading two files with names filename1 and filename2 that are given as inputs. The lengths of the files are stored in n and m. Then, a nested loop structure is used where the outer and inner loops are constructed for the numbers in the first and second files, respectively. If a number in the first file (vnumber) is the same as a number in the second file (wnumber), then a variable numberofmatches is incremented by one. Note that this variable is set to zero before the loops. Once the loops are completed, the lengths of the files and the number of matches are printed out (lines 16–18).

In the program above, it is quite possible to swap the loops so that the numbers in the first/second file can be considered in the outer/inner loop. Such a swap leads to the following program:

```
R Program: Comparing Numbers in Two Different Files (Revised)

01 comparenumbers = function(filename1,filename2){
02     v = strtoi(scan(filename1,"",quiet=TRUE))
03     w = strtoi(scan(filename2,"",quiet=TRUE))
04     n = length(v)
05     m = length(w)
06     numberofmatches = 0
07     for (j in 1:m){
08         wnumber = w[j]
09         for (i in 1:n){
10             vnumber = v[i]
11             if (wnumber == vnumber){
12                 numberofmatches = numberofmatches + 1
13             }
14         }
15     }
16     print(paste("Length of the first file:",n))
17     print(paste("Length of the second file:",m))
18     print(paste("Number of matches:",numberofmatches))
19 }
```

The programs above have almost the same efficiency, except a minor difference due to different numbers of executions of lines 08, i.e.,

$$vnumber = v[i]$$

and

$$wnumber = w[j]$$

in the first and second programs, respectively. Since these lines are not critical (only being inside the outer loop), one can expect that the programs work with the same processing time for large files.

The matching programs above have $\mathcal{O}(nm)$ time complexities, where n and m are file sizes, i.e., the numbers of elements in input files. Hence, for $m \approx n$, the processing time grows quadratically in terms of n. On the other hand, since it is assumed that input files contain numbers without any duplication, one can find faster ways to compare them and find the number of matches. For example, one can use the binary-search algorithm presented in Chap. 3. Specifically, given two files, each number in one of the files can be searched in the other one in logarithmic time. Then, for files of n numbers, this leads to a total of

$$n \times \mathcal{O}(\log n) = \mathcal{O}(n \log n)$$

time for searching/finding all numbers. In order to apply the binary-search algorithm, however, the searched vector should include sorted elements. Hence, before searching numbers, sorting is required that can be performed efficiently via the quick sort algorithm described in Chap. 6.

Considering the discussion above, the following program can be written for an efficient number matching between two files:

```
R Program: Comparing Numbers in Two Different Files Efficiently (Original)

01 comparenumberswithbs = function(filename1,filename2){
02     v = strtoi(scan(filename1,"",quiet=TRUE))
03     w = strtoi(scan(filename2,"",quiet=TRUE))
04     w = quicksort(w)
05     n = length(v)
06     m = length(w)
07     numberofmatches = 0
08     for (i in 1:n){
09         vnumber = v[i]
10         indexinfo = binarysearchrecursivemod(w,vnumber,1,m)
11         if (indexinfo != 0){
12             numberofmatches = numberofmatches + 1
13         }
14     }
15     print(paste("Length of the first file:",n))
16     print(paste("Length of the second file:",m))
17     print(paste("Number of matches:",numberofmatches))
18 }
```

Similar to the previous programs, the vectors v and w contain numbers in
filename1 and filename2, respectively. But, once w is formed, it is sorted
as

$$w = quicksort(w)$$

where we use the quick sort program presented in Chap. 6. As opposed to the previous programs, a single loop is constructed over the elements of v. Given an element
vnumber, it is searched inside w as

$$indexinfo = binarysearchrecursivemod(w,vnumber,1,m)$$

where indexinfo is the index of the searched number in w. For the binary search,
we use a modified version as follows:

```
R Program: Recursive Binary Search (Revised)

01 binarysearchrecursivemod = function(v,thenumber,lowerindex,higherindex){
02     if (lowerindex > higherindex){
03         return(0)
04     }
05     else{
06         middleindex = lowerindex + floor((higherindex-lowerindex)/2)
07         if (v[middleindex] == thenumber){
08             return(middleindex)
09         }
10         else if (v[middleindex] < thenumber){
11             binarysearchrecursive(v,thenumber,middleindex+1,higherindex)
12         }
13         else if (v[middleindex] > thenumber){
14             binarysearchrecursive(v,thenumber,lowerindex,middleindex-1)
15         }
16     }
17 }
```

Using the modified version of the binary search, line 10 of the main program returns zero if the number being searched is not found in the vector. Hence, following a search, the conditional statement

```
if (indexinfo != 0){
```

is used to check whether the number is found (`indexinfo` is a positive number) or not (`indexinfo` is zero).

Using the programs above and the quick sort program in Chap. 6, two files containing n numbers can be compared in a total of $\mathcal{O}(n \log n)$ time in average. This can be interpreted as a great reduction in the time complexity of number matching, considering the quadratic time complexity of the program based on direct comparisons.

8.4 Information Outputs

In some cases, output files are generated for information purposes, e.g., to keep records of runtime parameters such as timings or messages that are normally printed out. In R, such files can easily be generated using the built-in `sink` command, which directs the workspace into an output file. As an example, consider the following program that measures the processing time of matrix–vector multiplications for various random matrices and vectors of different sizes.

```
R Program: Checking Matrix–Vector Multiplication Time (Original)

01 checkmatvectime = function(infofile){
02     sink(infofile)
03     for (i in 1:5){
04         n = 100*i
05         A = matrix(rnorm(n*n,0,1),nrow=n)
06         x = matrix(rnorm(n,0,1),nrow=n)
07         print(paste("For n =",n,", system time is"))
08         print(system.time(matvecmult(A,x)))
09     }
10     sink()
11     print("Measurements are completed!")
12 }
```

For the matrix–vector multiplication in line 08, we use `matvecmult` presented in Chap. 4. The matrices and vectors are generated randomly in lines 05 and 06 as

```
A = matrix(rnorm(n*n,0,1),nrow=n)
```

and

```
x = matrix(rnorm(n,0,1),nrow=n)
```

respectively, where n takes values from 100 to 500. Using this program as

```
checkmatvectime("matvecinfo.txt")
```

creates a file matvecinfo.txt, which contains the outputs of lines 07 and 08. Specifically, the file contains five messages (due to print in line 07) and five timing outputs (due to `system.time` in line 08), leading to a total of 15 lines. These items, which are normally shown on the workspace, are written into a file since

```
sink(infofile)
```

is used before the loop. Here, `infofile` is a string input that specifies the file name. Finally, due to the `sink` command in line 10 without any input, the file is detached (but not deleted). Hence, the print command in line 11 leads to the message "Measurements are completed!" that appears on the workspace rather than the file.

8.5   Conclusions

As opposed to some other applications, file processing is quite dependent on the syntax of the programming language and requires it less algorithmic efforts. Hence, such programs implemented using a programming language may not be easily extended to other languages. Nevertheless, some common strategies need to be developed to investigate, process, and modify files. In some cases, multiple input and output files must be considered, while items in these files need to be processed quickly for efficient programming. One of the suggested projects in the final chapter requires some practices that require combinations of file processing, data processing, and computations, as commonly encountered in real-life applications.

8.6   Exercises

1. Write a program that investigates any given text file and prints out the total number of letters (i.e., characters other than spaces and punctuation marks). Test your program for various files.

2. Write a program that investigates any given text file and prints out the number of words starting with letter "a" or "A". Test your program for various files.

3. Write a program that investigates any given text file, selects words starting with letter "a' or "A", and writes the selected words into another file. Test your program for various files.

4. Write a program that investigates any given text file and generates a histogram for the number of words in sentences. Test your program for various files.

5. Write a program that modifies any given file containing numbers (in separate lines) by deleting some of its lines. Specifically, the program should delete the 2nd, 4th, 6th, ... lines, while keeping the 1st, 3rd, 5th, ... lines. Test your program for various files.

6. Write a program that mixes two given files containing numbers (in separate lines) into a single output file. Specifically, the program should read lines from the first and second files (input files) in a mixed order (i.e., one from the first file and the next from the second file) and write them into a third file (output file). Test your program for various files.

7. Use the sink command as `sink("mycomputations.txt")` to create a file. Then, perform some simple operations, such as additions and multiplications of numbers. Finally, use `sink()` to detach the file. Investigate the file by opening it in a text editor.

Suggested Mini Projects 9

This final chapter presents three mini projects suggested for better understanding of programming and some related concepts. In the first project, simple one-dimensional traffics are modeled based on given rules. In addition to some convergence analysis, processing times are measured and compared with theoretical estimations. The second project is related to sorting via the quick-sort algorithm. By writing some interface programs, we sort words in the alphabetical order. Finally, the third project focuses on linear systems of equations and their solutions with the Gaussian elimination. For the implementation of all projects, each student needs to select an id-number (can be derived from or be the same as her/his student number) involving nine digits, e.g., 200912345.

9.1 Programming Traffic

The aim of this project is to practice writing, testing, and modifying simple algorithms and their implementations. We consider one-dimensional traffic problems, whose solutions require iterations and analysis of convergence. We also measure the complexity of programs and algorithms and compare timing results with our estimations.

9.1.1 Preliminary Work

A one-dimensional traffic problem involves a one-way road of length n. We consider various roads with different lengths, assuming that n is a multiple of nine. Hence, choose an id-number with nine digits, e.g., 200912345.

Now, assume that we would like to initialize a traffic on a road of length $2 \times 9 = 18$. First, we write the id-number twice in a vector, i.e.,

$$v^0 = [2, 0, 0, 9, 1, 2, 3, 4, 5, 2, 0, 0, 9, 1, 2, 3, 4, 5].$$

Ö. Ergül, *Guide to Programming and Algorithms Using R*,
DOI 10.1007/978-1-4471-5328-3_9,
© Springer-Verlag London 2013

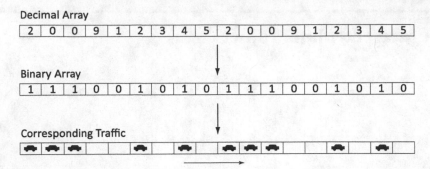

Fig. 9.1 An example to generate and interpret a traffic on a road of length 18

This is the decimal vector that represents the traffic. Then, we convert this vector into a binary vector by using 1 for even numbers and 0 for odd numbers. Hence, the corresponding binary vector is

$$b^0 = [1, 1, 1, 0, 0, 1, 0, 1, 0, 1, 1, 1, 0, 0, 1, 0, 1, 0].$$

Finally, this binary vector is converted into a meaningful traffic scenario. Specifically, the value 1 indicates that a car exists in a cell, whereas the value 0 indicates that the cell is empty. Note that there are a total of n cells, either empty or full (i.e., occupied by a car). Figure 9.1 depicts how to generate and interpret a traffic on a road of length 18.

A traffic that we generate as above is an initial ($t = 0$) condition, and we would like to see what happens in the next time steps, i.e., $t = 1, 2, 3, \ldots$. We assume that the traffic flows from left to right with the following simple rules:

- A car can move to the next cell (cell on the right) if the next cell is empty.
- A car cannot move to the next cell (cell on the right) if the next cell is full.
- A car in the last cell disappears in the next time step.

Before writing a program, it is essential to define the rules in an appropriate format. Since we are interested in the traffic on the road, the rules can be rewritten for each cell such that a decision chart in Table 9.1 is formed. In this decision chart, the status of the ith cell ($1 < i < n$) at time $t + 1$ is written depending on the status of the $(i - 1)$th, ith, and $(i + 1)$th cells at time t. For example, if $b^t[i - 1] = 1$, $b^t[i] = 0$, and $b^t[i + 1] = 1$ and as the time is incremented from t to $t + 1$, the car at the $(i - 1)$th cell moves to the ith cell, and we have $b^{t+1}[i] = 1$.

Table 9.1 clearly describes the evolution of the traffic as the time goes on. However, we can easily simplify it by investigating the values in detail. For example, consider $b^t[i] = 0$ (rows 1, 2, 5, and 6). In this case, we note that $b^{t+1}[i] = b^t[i - 1]$. This is because if the ith cell is empty at time t, its status at time $t + 1$ directly depends on the status of the previous cell at time t. Specifically, if the previous cell is empty, then there is no car to move to the ith cell, and the ith cell remains empty. If the previous cell is occupied by a car, however, that car moves to the ith cell at time $t + 1$. More importantly, all these movements do not depend on the status of the

Table 9.1 Decision chart for the one-dimensional traffic

$b^t[i-1]$	$b^t[i]$	$b^t[i+1]$	$b^{t+1}[i]$
0	0	0	0
0	0	1	0
0	1	0	0
0	1	1	1
1	0	0	1
1	0	1	1
1	1	0	0
1	1	1	1

Table 9.2 Short decision chart for the one-dimensional traffic

$b^t[i]$	$b^{t+1}[i]$
0	$b^t[i-1]$
1	$b^t[i+1]$

Table 9.3 Short decision chart for the first cell

$b^t[1]$	$b^{t+1}[1]$
0	0
1	$b^t[2]$

Table 9.4 Short decision chart for the last cell

$b^t[n]$	$b^{t+1}[n]$
0	$b^t[n-1]$
1	0

$(i+1)$th cell. By using this type of approaches, one can obtain the short decision chart in Table 9.2.

The decision chart in Table 9.2 (as well as in Table 9.1) is valid for $1 < i < n$ but not for $i = 1$ and $i = n$. At these boundary cells, separate rules listed in Tables 9.3 and 9.4 must be applied.

Figure 9.2 shows the evolution of the example binary vector from $t = 0$ to $t = 1$ and $t = 1$ to $t = 2$, as well as the corresponding traffic at $t = 2$.

9.1.2 Main Work 1

(1) Write a program (an R function called `initroad`) that generates a binary vector representing a traffic on a road of length $9m$, given the value of m. The program should generate the vector in accordance with the selected id-number. The output of the program should be this binary vector. Test your program for different values of m.

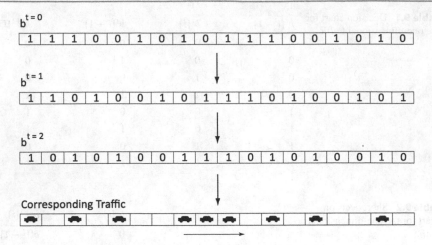

Fig. 9.2 Evolution of the traffic in Fig. 9.1 from $t = 0$ to $t = 2$

(2)   Write a program (an R function called `modifyroad`) that modifies a given
       binary vector according to the decision charts derived in the preliminary work.
       Specifically, the program should take a binary vector representing a traffic as
       input. The output should be another binary vector representing the traffic in
       the next time step. Test your program for various vectors.
(3)   Write a program (an R function called `countroad`) that counts the number
       of ones in a given binary vector. Hence, the output of the program should be
       the number of ones. Test your program for various vectors.
(4)   Using your programs, perform the following experiment:
       (a)   Generate a binary vector representing a traffic on a road of length 90
              ($m = 10$).
       (b)   Modify the binary vector and find the status of the traffic at $t =
              1, 2, 3, \ldots$. Each time step can be considered as an iteration. Perform
              iterations until the whole road is empty.
       (c)   Record the total number of cars at each time step in a file.
       (d)   Using the output file, make a plot displaying the number of cars as a
              function of time steps and observe how the number of cars decays to
              zero.
       An example plot is shown in Fig. 9.3.

9.1.3   Main Work 2

Consider again one-dimensional traffic problems while the rules at the boundary
cells are changed. Specifically, if there exists a car in the last cell, then, instead of
simply disappearing, it reenters the road from the first cell (if the first cell is already
empty) in the next time step. The decision charts for the boundary cells can be
revised as listed in Tables 9.5 and 9.6.

Fig. 9.3 Number of cars versus time steps

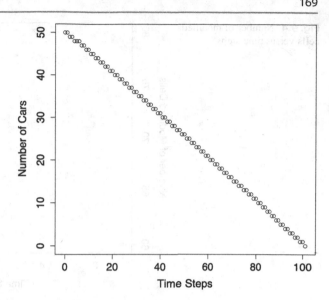

Table 9.5 Revised decision chart for the first cell

$b^t[1]$	$b^{t+1}[1]$
0	$b^t[n]$
1	$b^t[2]$

Table 9.6 Revised decision chart for the last cell

$b^t[n]$	$b^{t+1}[n]$
0	$b^t[n-1]$
1	$b^t[1]$

(1) Write a program (an R function called modifyroad2) that modifies a given binary vector according to the revised rules. Similar to the original program, the program should take a binary vector representing a traffic as input. The output should be another binary vector representing the traffic in the next time step. Test your program for various vectors.

(2) Write a program (an R function called compareroads) that compares two given binary vectors and returns the number cells with different values (zero in a vector and one in the other). Test your program for various pairs of vectors.

(3) Using your programs, perform the following experiment.
  (a) Generate a binary vector representing a traffic on a road of length 90 ($m = 10$).
  (b) Modify the binary vector and find the status of the traffic at $t = 1, 2, 3, \ldots$. Each time step can be considered as an iteration. Perform a total of 10 iterations.
  (c) Record the number of modified cells at each time step in a file.

Fig. 9.4 Number of modified cells versus time steps

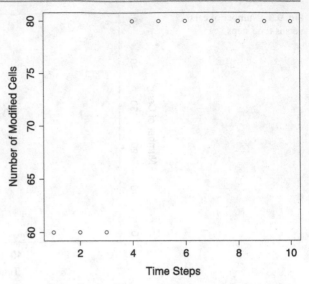

Table 9.7 Processing times required for modifying roads of different lengths

m	Measured (seconds)	Expected (seconds)
1000	0.040	–
2000	0.077	$2 \times 0.040 = 0.080$
4000	0.158	$4 \times 0.040 = 0.160$

(d) Using the output file, make a plot displaying the number of modified cells as a function of time steps and observe how the number of modified cells converges to a value (traffic speed) that depends on the number of empty cells on the road.

An example plot is shown in Fig. 9.4.

9.1.4 Main Work 3

Consider the solution of one-dimensional traffic problems with the revised rules.
(1) Find the order of the modification program theoretically.
(2) Generate a binary vector representing a traffic on a road of length 9000 ($m =$ 1000). Modify the binary vector and record the time required for this.
(3) Repeat items 1 and 2 for $m = 2000$.
(4) Repeat items 1 and 2 for $m = 4000$.
(5) Analyze your measurements (processing times for $m = 1000$, $m = 2000$, and $m = 4000$) considering the theoretical order of the modification program. A sample set of measurements is shown in Table 9.7.

Table 9.8 Conversion of the word "program" to an integer

Letters	p	r	o	g	r	a	m
Integers	16	18	15	7	18	1	13
Multiplier	27^6	27^5	27^4	27^3	27^2	27^1	27^0
Multiplication	6198727824	258280326	7971615	137781	13122	27	13

9.2 Sorting Words

In this project, we write and test some practical programs for reordering a given list of words according to the alphabetic order. For this purpose, we implement conversion functions between words and numbers, as well as the quick sort algorithm for the efficient sorting of numbers.

9.2.1 Preliminary Work

There can be different strategies to convert words to numbers and numbers to words. A valid conversion must be a one-to-one map between words and numbers, i.e., each word should correspond to a unique number and vice versa. In this project, we use a simple technique based on converting each letter to its order in the English alphabet. For example, "a" corresponds to 1, "b" corresponds to 2, "c" corresponds to 3, etc. To further simplify the conversion, we will assume that a word can have maximum seven letters.

As an example, consider the word "program" to be converted into a number. According to the alphabet, the numbers corresponding to the letters in "program" are 16 (for p), 18 (for r), 15 (for o), 7 (for g), 18 (for r), 1 (for a), and 13 (for m), respectively. In order to obtain a unique integer representation for "program", we multiply the first number corresponding to the first letter with 27^6, the second number corresponding to the second letter with 27^5, the third number corresponding to the third letter with 27^4, the fourth number corresponding to the fourth letter with 27^3, the fifth number corresponding to the fifth letter with 27^2, the sixth number corresponding to the sixth letter with 27^1, and the seventh number corresponding to the seventh letter with $27^0 = 1$. Then, we add the results of these multiplications to find the integer representation of the word. The operations performed for "program" are listed in Table 9.8. Note that "program" is uniquely represented by

$$6198727824 + 258280326 + 7971615 + 137781 + 13122 + 27 + 13 = 6465130708,$$

and no other word with seven letters is represented by the same integer.

The conversion described above also works well for words with less than seven letters. For example, consider the two-letter word "go". This word can be considered as a seven-letter word "go   ", with five spaces added at the end. When converting into numbers, the space character corresponds to the zero value. Since "g" and "o" are the 7th and 15th letters of the alphabet, the integer for the word "go" can be found as

$$7 \times 27^6 + 15 \times 27^5 + 0 \times 27^4 + 0 \times 27^3 + 0 \times 27^2 + 0 \times 27^1 + 0 \times 27^0 = 2927177028,$$

which is again a unique representation.

A conversion from words to numbers can be meaningful only when a reverse conversion exists. Specifically, a method to convert numbers back to words is required. Using the technique above, the reverse conversion can be described as follows. For a given integer i, apply the steps consecutively.

- The number corresponding to the first letter can be found as $\lfloor i/27^6 \rfloor$, where $\lfloor \cdot \rfloor$ represents the floor operation. In other words, $\lfloor i/27^6 \rfloor$ is the order of the first letter in the alphabet.
- Do $i = i - \lfloor i/27^6 \rfloor \times 27^6$. If the result is greater than zero, then there is a second letter, and its order in the alphabet is $\lfloor i/27^5 \rfloor$.
- Do $i = i - \lfloor i/27^5 \rfloor \times 27^5$. If the result is greater than zero, then there is a third letter, and its order in the alphabet is $\lfloor i/27^4 \rfloor$.
- Do $i = i - \lfloor i/27^4 \rfloor \times 27^4$. If the result is greater than zero, then there is a fourth letter, and its order in the alphabet is $\lfloor i/27^3 \rfloor$.
- Do $i = i - \lfloor i/27^3 \rfloor \times 27^3$. If the result is greater than zero, then there is a fifth letter, and its order in the alphabet is $\lfloor i/27^2 \rfloor$.
- Do $i = i - \lfloor i/27^2 \rfloor \times 27^2$. If the result is greater than zero, then there is a sixth letter, and its order in the alphabet is $\lfloor i/27^1 \rfloor$.
- Do $i = i - \lfloor i/27^1 \rfloor \times 27^1$. If the result is greater than zero, then there is a seventh letter, and its order in the alphabet is $\lfloor i/27^0 \rfloor = \lfloor i \rfloor$.

As an example, lets apply this algorithm to $i = 6465130708$. It can be found that $\lfloor i/27^6 \rfloor = 16$, and we continue as follows:

- $i = i - 16 \times 27^6 = 266402884$ and $\lfloor i/27^5 \rfloor = 18$.
- $i = i - 18 \times 27^5 = 8122558$ and $\lfloor i/27^4 \rfloor = 15$.
- $i = i - 15 \times 27^4 = 150943$ and $\lfloor i/27^3 \rfloor = 7$.
- $i = i - 7 \times 27^3 = 13162$ and $\lfloor i/27^2 \rfloor = 18$.
- $i = i - 18 \times 27^2 = 40$ and $\lfloor i/27^1 \rfloor = 1$.
- $i = i - 1 \times 27^1 = 13$ and $\lfloor i/27^0 \rfloor = 13$.

Hence, the numbers corresponding to the letters are $\{16,18,15,7,18,1,13\}$, and the represented word is "program".

Next, consider the integer $i = 2927177028$. One can find that $\lfloor i/27^6 \rfloor = 7$. Updating as

$$i = i - \lfloor i/27^6 \rfloor \times 27^6 = 215233605,$$

the next value is $\lfloor i/27^5 \rfloor = 15$. Then, the next update, i.e.,

$$i - \lfloor i/27^5 \rfloor \times 27^5 = 0,$$

leads to a zero value. Hence, after this point, there is no need to continue. The numbers are $\{7,15,0,0,0,0,0\}$, and the corresponding word is "go   ".

9.2.2 Main Work 1

(1) Write a program (an R function called `charactertointeger`) that converts a given letter from "a" to "z" to an integer from 1 to 26. The program should take a string of one character as an input. The output should be an integer (1–26) depending on the order of the letter in the English alphabet. The program should return zero for the space character.

(2) Write a program (an R function called `wordtointeger`) that converts a given word to an integer using the rules described in the preliminary work. The program should take a string of seven letters and give an integer (unique representation of the word) as the output. The program should use `charactertointeger` implemented in item 1. Test your program for various words with different lengths.

(3) Write a program (an R function called `integertocharacter`) that converts a given integer 1 to 26 to a letter from "a" to "z". The program should take an integer as an input. The output should be a string of one character depending on the integer (order in the English alphabet). The program should return the space character for a zero input.

(4) Write a program (an R function called `integertoword`) that converts a given integer to a word using the rules described in the preliminary work. The program should take an integer as an input. The output should be a string of seven characters. The program should use `integertocharacter` implemented in item 3. Test your program for various integers, including 2972915217, 4876069590, 2461131702, 3321154924.

9.2.3 Main Work 2

(1) Generate/write a file of 100 words. The file should be readable in the R environment. Each word should be written as a new line, i.e., the file should contain 100 lines. Each word should contain maximum seven letters. If a word contains less than seven letters, space characters should be added at the end.

(2) Write a program that sorts the elements of a given vector using the quick sort algorithm. Specifically, the program should take a vector of integers as an input. The output should be another or the same vector with sorted elements (in the ascending order). Use $p = \lfloor n/2 \rfloor$ as the pivoting strategy. Test your function for various vectors with different sizes and elements.

(3) Using your programs, perform the following.
   (a) Read the data file including 100 words. Put the words into a vector ("word vector") of 100 elements.
   (b) Convert each word in the "word vector" into an integer. Put the integers into a vector ("number vector") of 100 elements.
   (c) Sort the "number vector" using the quick sort algorithm. Generate a "sorted number vector".

(d) Convert each integer in the "sorted number vector" into a word. Put the
     words into a vector ("sorted word vector") of 100 elements.

(e) Write the words in the "sorted word vector" into a data file. Open the
     data file generated by the script. Investigate the file carefully and make
     sure that words in the input data file are sorted correctly according to
     the alphabetic order.

9.3   Designing Systems

In this project, we focus on writing programs to solve linear systems of equations.
Specifically, we consider the Gaussian elimination without pivoting and with partial
pivoting to solve matrix equations. Solutions can be interpreted as inputs that are
required to generate a given set of outputs from a linear system.

9.3.1   Preliminary Work

Consider a linear system involving n inputs and n outputs as depicted in Fig. 9.5.
This system may represent a real-life instrument, such as a linear electronic circuit,
where the inputs and outputs are electrical signals.

In this project, we consider relatively small linear systems involving 9×9 matrix equations. The matrix elements will be determined by using an id-number as
follows. Let the id-number be 200912345. Then, the first row of the matrix consists
of 2, 0, 0, 9, 1, 2, 3, 4, and 5, respectively. The next row involves the same numbers with a shift to the right, i.e., 5, 2, 0, 0, 9, 1, 2, 3, 4. Note that the last element
in the first row is moved to the beginning of the sequence in the second row. The
subsequent rows are formed similarly with regular shifts, leading to a 9×9 matrix
as

$$
A = \begin{bmatrix}
2 & 0 & 0 & 9 & 1 & 2 & 3 & 4 & 5 \\
5 & 2 & 0 & 0 & 9 & 1 & 2 & 3 & 4 \\
4 & 5 & 2 & 0 & 0 & 9 & 1 & 2 & 3 \\
3 & 4 & 5 & 2 & 0 & 0 & 9 & 1 & 2 \\
2 & 3 & 4 & 5 & 2 & 0 & 0 & 9 & 1 \\
1 & 2 & 3 & 4 & 5 & 2 & 0 & 0 & 9 \\
9 & 1 & 2 & 3 & 4 & 5 & 2 & 0 & 0 \\
0 & 9 & 1 & 2 & 3 & 4 & 5 & 2 & 0 \\
0 & 0 & 9 & 1 & 2 & 3 & 4 & 5 & 2
\end{bmatrix}.
$$

We consider matrix equations involving the matrix derived above (as well as a modified version) and different right-hand-side vectors.

The aim of the project is as follows. We would like to design a system that can
provide a predetermined set of outputs in a controllable manner. Since the matrix elements are determined as above, the matrix representing the system is already fixed.
However, one can control the output by adjusting the input. Hence, our purpose is

Fig. 9.5 A system involving
n inputs and n outputs

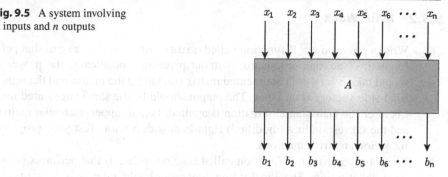

to find the required set of inputs to obtain a given set of outputs. This requires the solution of the matrix equations involving the matrix above.

As an example, assume that we would like to find the input values for an output vector

$$b^{(1)} = \begin{bmatrix} 1 \\ 0 \\ 0 \\ 0 \\ 0 \\ 0 \\ 0 \\ 0 \\ 0 \end{bmatrix}.$$

Solving the matrix equation

$$Ax^{(1)} = b^{(1)}$$

gives

$$x^{(1)} = \begin{bmatrix} -3.99 \\ -7.93 \\ -8.39 \\ 5.72 \\ 0.25 \\ 5.89 \\ 7.52 \\ 4.00 \\ 1.30 \end{bmatrix} \times 10^{-2}$$

with three digits of accuracy. In other words, $x^{(1)}$ is the input required to produce $b^{(1)}$ as the output. Matrix equations involving a 9×9 matrix and a few right-hand-side vectors can be solved by using the Gaussian elimination. Note that, for larger matrices, the LU factorization would be better since a single decomposition of a matrix is sufficient for all solutions with different right-hand-side vectors.

9.3.2   Main Work 1

(1) Write a program (an R function called `gaussianelimination`) that performs the Gaussian elimination without pivoting. Specifically, the program should take $n \times (n+1)$ augmented matrix (including the matrix and the right-hand-side vector) as an input. The output should be the same augmented matrix after the Gaussian elimination is applied, i.e., an upper-triangular matrix and the corresponding (modified) right-hand-side vector. Test your program for various matrix equations.

(2) Write a program (an R function called `backwardsub`) that performs backward substitution. Specifically, the program should take an $n \times n$ upper-triangular matrix and a right-hand-side vector (they can be augmented, if desired) as inputs. The output should be the solution vector. Test your function for various matrix equations.

(3) Using your programs, perform the following.

    (a) Generate a matrix equation involving a 9×9 matrix. The matrix elements should be determined as described in the preliminary work. Select an arbitrary right-hand-side vector involving only ones and zeros.

    (b) Apply the Gaussian elimination without pivoting to the matrix equation.

    (c) Apply the backward substitution to find the solution of the matrix equation.

    (d) Print out the solution. Note that it contains the input values required to generate the desired output values.

    (e) Check the solution by multiplying it with the matrix and comparing the result with the right-hand-side vector. Is there any error? Why?

9.3.3   Main Work 2

(1) Write a program (an R function called `gaussianelimination partial`) that performs the Gaussian elimination with partial pivoting. Specifically, the program should take $n \times (n+1)$ augmented matrix (including the matrix and the right-hand-side vector) as an input. The output should be the same augmented matrix after the Gaussian elimination with partial pivoting is applied, i.e., an upper-triangular matrix and the corresponding (modified) right-hand-side vector. Test your program for various matrix equations.

(2) Using your programs, perform the following.

    (a) Generate a matrix equation involving a 9×9 matrix. The matrix elements should be determined as described in the preliminary work, but with the following modification: Set the diagonal elements to zero. Use the right-hand-side vector that you use in Main Work 1.

    (b) Apply the Gaussian elimination without pivoting to the matrix equation.

    (c) Apply the backward substitution to find the solution of the matrix equation.

    (d) Print out the solution. What happened?

(3)　Using your programs, perform the following.
  (a)　Generate a matrix equation involving a 9×9 matrix. The matrix elements should be determined as described in the preliminary work, but with the following modification: Set the diagonal elements to zero. Use the right-hand-side vector that you use in Main Work 1.
  (b)　Apply the Gaussian elimination with partial pivoting to the matrix equation.
  (c)　Apply the backward substitution to find the solution of the matrix equation.
  (d)　Print out the solution. Note that it contains the input values required to generate the desired output values.
  (e)　Check the solution by multiplying it with the matrix and comparing the result with the right-hand-side vector. Is there any error? Why?

Bibliography

1. Aho AV, Hopcroft JE, Ullman JD (1974) The design and analysis of computer algorithms. Addison-Wesley, Reading
2. Dijkstra EW (1976) A discipline of programming. Prentice Hall, New York
3. Wirth N (1976) Algorithms + data structures = programs. Prentice Hall, New York
4. Aho AV, Ullman JD, Hopcroft JE (1983) Data structures and algorithms. Addison-Wesley, Reading
5. Roberts ES (1986) Thinking recursively. Wiley, New York
6. Shackelford RL (1997) Introduction to computing and algorithms. Addison-Wesley, Reading
7. Bentley J (1999) Programming Pearls. Addison-Wesley, Reading
8. Lafore R (2002) Data structures and algorithms in Java. Sams, Indianapolis
9. Johnsonbaugh R, Schaefer M (2003) Algorithms. Prentice Hall, New York
10. Skiena SS, Revilla M (2003) Programming challenges. Springer, Berlin
11. Lee RCT, Tseng SS, Chang RC, Tsai YT (2005) Introduction to the design and analysis of algorithms. McGraw-Hill, New York
12. Kleinberg J, Tardos E (2005) Algorithm design. Addison-Wesley, Reading
13. Dasgupta S, Papadimitriou C, Vazirani U (2006) Algorithms. McGraw-Hill, New York
14. Levitin A (2006) Introduction to the design and analysis of algorithms. Addison-Wesley, Reading
15. McConnell J (2007) Analysis of algorithms. Jones & Bartlett, Boston
16. Sedgewick R, Wayne K (2007) Introduction to programming in Java: an interdisciplinary approach. Addison-Wesley, Reading
17. Skiena SS (2008) The algorithm design manual. Springer, Berlin
18. Heineman GT, Pollice G, Selkow S (2008) Algorithms in a nutshell. O'Reilly Media, Sebastopol
19. Wang W (2008) Beginning programming all-in-one desk reference for dummies. For Dummies, New York
20. Cormen TH, Leiserson CE, Rivest RL, Stein C (2009) Introduction to algorithms. MIT Press, Cambridge
21. Soltys M (2009) An introduction to the analysis of algorithms. World Scientific, Singapore
22. Shen A (2010) Algorithms and programming. Springer, Berlin
23. Bird R (2010) Pearls of functional algorithm design. Cambridge University Press, Cambridge
24. Knuth DE (2011) The art of computer programming. Addison-Wesley, Reading
25. Sedgewick R, Wayne K (2011) Algorithms. Addison-Wesley, Reading
26. Karumanchi N (2011) Data structures and algorithms made easy: data structure and algorithmic puzzles. CreateSpace, New York
27. Shaffer CA (2011) Data structures and algorithm analysis in Java. Dover, New York

28. Chivers I, Sleightholme J (2012) Introduction to programming with Fortran: with coverage of Fortran 90, 95, 2003, 2008 and 77. Springer, Berlin
29. Crawley MJ (2012) The R book. Wiley, New York
30. Sedgewick R, Flajolet P (2013) An introduction to the analysis of algorithms. Addison-Wesley, Reading

Index

Ö. Ergül, *Guide to Programming and Algorithms Using R*,
DOI 10.1007/978-1-4471-5328-3,
© Springer-Verlag London 2013

Printed in the United States
By Bookmasters